The Wedding Workbook

The Wedding Workbook

Bette Matthews

FRIEDMAN/FAIRFAX
PUBLISHERS

A FRIEDMAN/FAIRFAX BOOK

Library of Congress Cataloging-in-Publication data available upon request.

1-56799-755-4

Editor: Ann Kirby
Art Director: Jeff Batzli
Designer and Illustrator: Kirsten Berger
Production Director: Karen Matsu Greenberg

Color separations by Bright Arts Graphics, Pte. Ltd.
Printed in Singapore

5 7 9 10 8 6 4

For bulk purchases and special sales, please contact:
Friedman/Fairfax Publishers
Attention: Sales Department
15 West 26th Street
New York, New York 10010
212/685-6610   FAX 212/685-1307

Visit our website:
www.metrobooks.com

To Antonio

Joined, we are strong.

Contents

Introduction

Congratulations. He asked and you said yes, or vice versa, or maybe you just looked at each other one day and asked "Why not?" And now you can plan to spend the rest of your lives together. But before you do, you have a wedding to plan, and right about now you may be wondering where to start.

Planning a wedding is one of the most complicated events most people will ever have to orchestrate. It can be simultaneously joyous and frustrating. Many brides, and some grooms, have a very clear vision of what their dream wedding will be, while others have given it little thought prior to becoming engaged. One way or the other, you are about to be inundated with information and opinions, recommendations and decisions.

But don't panic. Planning your wedding with as little stress as possible is simply a matter of staying organized. And that's just what *The Wedding Workbook* will help you to do. In this book, you can find all the steps you will need to take, all the details you will need to coordinate, and a place to keep your records and check your schedule. It is also filled with ideas, both traditional and modern, to help you create a wedding that captures your personality and style.

Your engagement is your first step towards marriage. During this time you will be basking in the glow of your commitment and the warm wishes of everyone you know. And as you plan your wedding, you will learn to negotiate, compromise, accommodate, choose, and stand by your decisions—all of which make for a good rehearsal for married life. In fact, unlike many wedding planners, this workbook is addressed to both the bride and the groom, because planning your wedding should be a joint venture, a prelude to the life you'll share afterward. So take a deep breath and get ready for an adventure. You've made the decision to wed. Now comes the hard part. Saying yes is only the beginning.

Chapter One

Spreading the News

Now that the decision is made, it is time to make it official. Sharing your news with family and friends is the first step you'll take toward uniting your lives and will be your first taste of all the fun, and, yes, frustration that will go into planning your wedding.

Getting the Word Out

Letting friends and family know can be the most exciting part of your engagement. However, it can also be the first place to trip up on etiquette or find yourself in an awkward situation. People will be thrilled to hear your news, but some can be easily hurt if they hear it through the grapevine rather than directly from you. Figure out who needs to know first, and who can be told a bit later. Start by making a list to ensure that no one is overlooked.

Tell your closest family members first, and tell them in person. The first to receive the news should be the people whose lives will be most touched by your plans. If either of you has children, share the news with them first, and be prepared for plenty of questions. Your parents should also be among those told first, if at all possible, visit them in person, and perhaps plan a casual lunch at a restaurant near their homes.

Start making calls. People are always thrilled to hear happy news and want to know right away. Start off by calling your closest friends and be sure to let them know whether it's okay if they spread the word to others, or if you'd rather handle it yourself.

Delegate! Split the list up between bride and groom, have your parents call the family, and recruit your best friends to spread the news to your college buddies.

Start writing notes. A handwritten note or letter is a more formal method of informing friends and family of your betrothal, yet still has a personal touch. It is a great way to get the news to friends with whom you were once close but perhaps have lost touch. If possible, take advantage of the efficiency of e-mail, a time-saving convenience.

Formal announcements. Sending out formal announcements is customary in certain social circles but is frowned upon in others because it may be viewed as a plea for gifts.

Tips

As soon as the deed is done, prepare for an onslaught of questions. Will it be a short engagement or a long one? Will you have an intimate cocktail party at a friend's elegant home, a gala dinner dance in a hotel ballroom, perhaps a barbecue in the backyard of the family home? Many newly engaged couples have not yet thought about the types of decisions they will have to make, let alone had the opportunity to discuss them. You will be amazed at how much unsolicited advice you are about to receive. Take a deep breath, put on your most congenial smile, and remember that all these people love you. They are excited about your marriage and want to offer their experience in order to help you. During your engagement you will probably fine-tune the art of being gracious.

Celebrating the News

Now that the news is out, be prepared for a period of constant celebrations. From informal gatherings with friends to shop for dresses to elaborate engagement parties, the pre-wedding festivities will abound. In the early part of your engagement, there are a few traditions you might want to consider.

Introduce your parents. Traditionally, the groom's parents first call the bride's parents to express their happiness at the news of their children's engagement. The bride's parents then host a gathering for the groom's parents. But don't feel bound by tradition. If the bride's parents want to make the first call, let them have the pleasure, or if you prefer, host a gathering to introduce them all yourselves.

The engagement party. Usually hosted by the bride's family, an engagement party can be as formal or informal as you wish. You can use it as an opportunity to announce your engagement to family and friends or, if you have already spread the news, simply as a celebration of your decision. Gifts are not commonly given at an engagement party. However, if you receive one, be sure to send a thank-you note promptly.

Newspaper Announcements

Placing an announcement in your local paper may be done at any point after your engagement up to several weeks before the wedding, when you are ready to send out invitations. If you have an idea of the date for your wedding, by all means include it. Most newspapers have a standard format for such announcements, and will want you to follow their instructions.

Examples of traditional wordings follow. Use **Worksheet 1** to work out the particular details of your announcement.

Announcement by the bride's parents. Simply reverse the announcement order if this is to be made by the groom's parents.

> *Mr. and Mrs. Charles Millard Smith of Putnam, Connecticut, announce the engagement of their daughter, Lucille May, to Mr. Jonathan Rose, the son of Mr. and Mrs. James Rose of Newport, Rhode Island. A June wedding is planned.*

Announcement by a widowed parent. You should include the name of a deceased parent in the newspaper announcement.

> *Mrs. Charles Millard Smith of Putnam, Connecticut, announces the engagement of her daughter, Lucille May, to Mr. Jonathan Rose, the son of Mr. and Mrs. James Rose of Newport, Rhode Island. Miss Smith is also the daughter of the late Mr. Charles Millard Smith. A June wedding is planned.*

Divorced parents. Divorced parents can announce the marriage together, either with or without the inclusion of second spouses. For divorced parents who have not remarried, the wording might be as follows.

> *Mr. Charles Millard Smith and Ms. Katherine Smith announce the engagement of their daughter, Lucille May, to Mr. Jonathan Rose, the son of Mr. and Mrs. James Rose of Newport, Rhode Island. A June wedding is planned.*

For divorced parents who have remarried, the wording would be similar, using the parents' individual surnames.

> *Mr. Charles Millard Smith and Mrs. Steven Beatty announce the engagement of their daughter, Lucille May, to Mr. Jonathan Rose, the son of Mr. and Mrs. James Rose of Newport, Rhode Island. A June wedding is planned.*

When a single divorced parent wishes to make the announcement, he or she may choose whether or not to include the name of his or her former spouse.

Mr. Charles Millard Smith announces the engagement of his daughter, Lucille May, to Mr. Jonathan Rose, the son of Mr. and Mrs. James Rose of Newport, Rhode Island. Miss Smith is also the daughter of Ms. Katherine Smith. A June wedding is planned.

Announcement by a parent and stepparent. If a stepparent has played an integral role in the bride's life, the announcement might read as follows.

Mr. and Mrs. Steven Beatty announce the engagement of Mrs. Beatty's daughter, Lucille May Smith, to Mr. Jonathan Rose, the son of Mr. and Mrs. James Rose of Newport, Rhode Island. Miss Smith is also the daughter of Mr. Charles Millard Smith. A June wedding is planned.

Announcement by the couple. Many couples wish to make the announcement themselves. Such an announcement may or may not include parents' names.

Miss Lucille May Smith of Putnam, Connecticut, and Mr. Jonathan Rose of Newport, Rhode Island, are pleased to announce their engagement. Miss Smith is the daughter of Mr. and Mrs. Charles Millard Smith of Putnam, Connecticut. Mr. Rose is the son of Mr. and Mrs. James Rose of Newport, Rhode Island. A June wedding is planned.

Worksheet 1: Your Newspaper Announcement

If you choose to announce your engagement in your local newspapers, use this worksheet to keep track of pertinent information and to figure out the wording.

Newspaper _____

Address _____

Telephone _____

Contact _____

Deadline _____

Fee _____

Photo _____

Your desired wording

_____

_____

_____

_____

_____

_____

_____

_____

_____

The Support Group: Your Wedding Party

Whatever the size of your celebration, you will want to be surrounded by those closest to you, and you will need help. Enter the wedding party. Some brides and grooms choose to have just one honor attendant each, while others may want an entourage of a dozen or more. Although a wedding party of such large proportions usually indicates an equally large and formal wedding, ultimately the decision on the number of attendants should reflect your wishes to include your loved ones in this important event.

Asking someone to be this involved in your wedding is an honor that should be bestowed judiciously, and a responsibility that will be accepted in the same manner. Keep in mind that there are extra costs for the people in the wedding party— bridesmaids' gowns and accessories, tuxedo rentals, parties thrown in your honor, extra traveling for fittings and rehearsals—all of which are added to the standard expenses of attending a wedding. If someone declines your invitation, try not to take it personally. Remember that there are financial, emotional, and time commitments that an attendant must be willing to accept. Declining to take on the responsibility of being in your wedding party is not a rejection of you but an honest answer to a well-considered issue.

Tips

As a general guideline, the children in your wedding party should be at least four years of age. Younger children may be included, though you run a higher risk of unpredictability. Little Maya may feel frightened in front of an unfamiliar group of people; Ivy might decide this is a good opportunity to show off how well she does a cartwheel; and young Ricky could just sit down in the middle of the aisle and wail. Small children have certainly been included in many weddings and carried out their duties without a hitch, but it's best to be prepared for the unexpected when the day arrives.

Maid or matron of honor. This honor is usually offered to your closest friend or relative, your sister, or even your mother. Some women choose a male friend or brother to stand up for them, who could then be called the man of honor or simply the honor attendant. It is not uncommon to have two maids of honor, or a maid and a matron, but you will have to decide which duties are assigned to each.

Your maid of honor assists you in any phase of wedding planning that you request, which may include shopping for dresses with you, pre-screening any of the wedding vendors, and addressing invitations. The maid of honor may host or organize a bridal shower for you, and may organize a bachelorette party as well. On your wedding day, she holds the ring you will give to your groom, holds your bouquet and arranges your train during the ceremony, and signs your marriage certificate as a witness. During the reception, she may give a toast.

Best man. This is the groom's closest relative or friend, and could be his father or grandfather. Some grooms who are very close to more than one person choose to have two best men. Or, a groom may choose a close female friend or a sister to stand up for him, and she is commonly referred to as best woman or honor attendant.

The best man arranges the bachelor party and may help the groom make the honeymoon arrangements. He arrives early on the day of the wedding to help the groom with whatever is required, including getting him to the ceremony on time. Like the maid of honor, the best man also signs the marriage certificate as a witness and holds the bride's ring until the groom is ready to place it on her finger. It is the honor of the best man to offer the first toast to the bride and groom.

Bridesmaids. If the maid of honor is the sergeant of your support system, the bridesmaids are the troops. Chosen based on the closeness of your relationship, they can help you with various small tasks during planning stages, and may share the expense and organization of your bridal shower with the maid of honor.

Junior bridesmaids are usually between the ages of nine and fourteen. Depending on the style of dress chosen, they may wear either the same dress or something similar to, but less mature than, the other bridesmaids' dresses.

Ushers/groomsmen. Chosen from among the groom's close friends and relatives, ushers may help the best man with arrangements for the bachelor party. An usher's main job is to seat guests at the ceremony, offering his right arm to a woman or simply escorting a man to an available seat on either the bride's or groom's side. For practical purposes, you will want one usher for every fifty guests, but don't feel that you have to limit yourself if you want to have more groomsmen. The ushers may have to roll out an aisle runner or loosen pew ribbons. One will be designated to escort the bride's mother to and from her seat if she is not a part of the processional.

Junior ushers are usually between nine and fourteen years of age and can have the same duties, or they can be stationed near the door to hand out wedding programs. The ushers should arrive at the ceremony site approximately one hour before the service begins.

Flower girl. This duty is generally given to a child between the ages of four and nine. She carries a basket of flowers or petals to scatter in the aisle before the bride walks down to meet the groom, making a beautiful path for her to follow.

Ring bearer. Again, this is a child aged four to nine, who carries the rings down the aisle on a decorative pillow. Traditionally the ring bearer is a boy, but nowadays girls are also chosen for this job. Depending on the age of the child, the rings on the pillow may be symbolic, leaving the maid of honor and best man to hold the actual wedding rings; with an older child, the actual rings may be entrusted. In either case, make sure the rings are fastened securely to the pillow.

Pages. Sometimes used in a very formal wedding, these children help carry the bride's long train down the aisle. Pages usually come in pairs, one stationed on each side of the train. Again, boys are the traditional choice but today girls are used as pages as well.

Spreading the News

Chapter Two

Preliminary Planning & Budgeting

Now it's time to get down to business There are numerous details that will require your attention during this process, but first you must concentrate on the big issues, such as the date, the location, and the budget. As you consider options and costs, keep in mind that there are many factors that will affect your planning, such as your personal style, the expectations of your parents and families, and whether the timing will conflict with your jobs in any way or interfere with other upcoming events or holidays.

Communication will be a key element throughout the planning stages. A wedding is never about one person only, but rather a celebration that reflects the tastes, visions, and pocketbooks of all involved parties. It is best to discuss all concerns openly with each other and your families.

Below is an overview of what you will need to accomplish. Within each category of this fairly simple list are myriad details to be attended to and decisions to be made. So get ready to work.

- ☐ Set the budget
- ☐ Choose the date and time
- ☐ Select your attendants
- ☐ Delegate responsibilities to others
- ☐ Hire a wedding consultant
- ☐ Book the ceremony site and officiant
- ☐ Book the reception site and caterer
- ☐ Hire the photographer and videographer
- ☐ Hire a florist
- ☐ Arrange music for the ceremony and reception
- ☐ Hire a baker for the wedding cake (if not included with catering)
- ☐ Arrange transportation
- ☐ Decide wedding style and colors
- ☐ Buy your wedding apparel

- [ ] Buy wedding rings
- [ ] Register for gifts
- [ ] Shop for your attendants' attire
- [ ] Compile your guest list
- [ ] Order invitations
- [ ] Address and mail invitations
- [ ] Purchase gifts for your attendants
- [ ] Get blood tests and marriage license
- [ ] Organize bridesmaids' party
- [ ] Create seating chart
- [ ] Schedule rehearsal
- [ ] Organize your honeymoon plans

Budget Preliminaries

Deciding on a budget will be one of the most critical steps in planning your wedding. Determining how much you will spend directly affects all of the miscellaneous details. Your first step will be an open discussion with your families to find out if they will be contributing to the wedding, and the amount of their contribution. Based on what you and/or your families can afford, arrive at a total figure, and make that your limit.

Who pays? Traditionally, the bride's family pays for the majority of the costs involved. Today it is common for the groom's family to add to the wedding coffer as well, and in many cases the bride and groom choose to pay for all wedding expenses themselves. According to tradition, expenses were divided as follows:

The Bride's Family

+ groom's ring
+ all stationery and postage
+ wedding gift for the groom
+ gifts for the bride's attendants
+ lodging for the bride's
  out-of-town attendants
+ bridesmaids' party
+ bride's attire and trousseau
+ flowers for female attendants

The Groom's Family

+ bride's rings
+ wedding gift for the bride
+ marriage license
+ officiant's fee
+ groom's attire
+ gifts for groom's attendants
+ lodging for groom's
  out-of-town attendants
+ bride's bouquet

The Bride's Family

+ photography and videography
+ fees for ceremony site
+ decorations/flowers for the ceremony site
+ music for ceremony and reception
+ transportation
+ fees for reception, including site rental, food, beverages, and gratuities
+ decorations for reception
+ any miscellaneous reception fees, such as valet parking and coat check

The Groom's Family

+ corsages for mothers
+ boutonnières for men in wedding party
+ rehearsal dinner
+ honeymoon

Nowadays, however, it is more common for families to simply contribute a set amount to the overall budget and allow the bride and groom to spend it as they wish. There are no longer any rules that haven't been broken. The bottom line is that you must come to a realistic budget for all concerned. No one should feel they have to contribute more than they can afford. Whatever your budget, with proper planning and care, you will be able to put together a lovely wedding that you can cherish your entire life.

Once you've determined how much money you have to work with, remember that reception costs will eat up 50 percent of your total budget, and that photography, music, flowers, attire, and miscellaneous expenses can be estimated at 10 percent each. Of course, these numbers are flexible; if you want to spend more money on a specific detail, the budget can still work if you trim costs in another area. There are a number of major decisions that will affect the cost of your wedding and will need serious consideration.

Style and formality. Whether you have always dreamed of a cathedral wedding followed by a black-tie dinner/dance reception or a simple ceremony in your parents' house followed by a backyard barbecue, determining the type of wedding you want will influence how much you will have to spend to see your dream fulfilled.

Location. Costs vary greatly in different parts of the country, and sometimes moving your reception to another city (perhaps where either of you grew up or went to school) can cut or increase your expenses significantly. Additionally, there can be a wide variety of options and a wide range of fees at diverse locations in your local area, so do your homework and compare.

Number of guests. There are many fixed costs in a wedding, such as music, photography, and attire. But other fees increase as your guest list increases. Working out your guest list—and all the costs involved—will be discussed later in this chapter.

Timing. At many reception halls, the time of year, day of the week, and even time of day can affect the costs of your wedding. Options and costs will be discussed later in this chapter.

Length of engagement. The longer you have to plan, the more opportunities you will have for comparison shopping, which can save you a lot of money in the long run. When making your arrangements far in advance, you have the pick of the playing field—wedding professionals have not yet booked up the most desirable dates, and you can look at a wide range of choices before making yours. With a shorter engagement, you may need to be willing to compromise on some of your choices, and you must be able to act quickly.

Worksheet 2: Estimating Your Budget

Use this worksheet to calculate the budget for your wedding. Starting with the total amount you want to spend, work backward to figure out how much you can spend on each item. Making sure to call different sources to get accurate estimates, start by filling out your initial estimates in column one. Add up the amounts and see where you are. Over budget? You can take this opportunity to make changes and eliminate certain details in order to cut costs. Put your new estimates in column two. Later on, as you make decisions and book services, write the actual costs into column three to keep track of your expenditures.

Item	Estimate #1	Estimate #2	Actual costs
Bridal gown and trousseau; include hair and makeup if you plan on having it done professionally			
Bridesmaids' party			
Decorations for reception			
Favors for guests at reception			
Fees for ceremony site			
Flowers for church, reception hall, attendants, and parents			
Gifts for bridal party			
Gift baskets for guests from out-of-town			
Groom's attire			
Honeymoon			
Marriage license, physical exams, and blood tests, if necessary			
Music for ceremony			
Music for reception			

Item	Estimate #1	Estimate #2	Actual costs
Officiant's fee			
Photography and videography			
Reception fees, including site rental, food, beverages, and gratuities			
Rehearsal dinner			
Rings for bride and groom			
Invitations and thank-you notes, as well as postage for same			
Transportation for wedding party, and guests if necessary			
Wedding gifts for one another			
Miscellaneous reception fees, such as valet parking and coat check			
TOTAL BUDGET			

Setting the Date

It all seems more official once you've chosen a date. There are, however, many factors to consider, including the budget, the time you'll need to plan, the weather, even the style of dress and flowers that you prefer. Remember that Saturday night is generally the most sought-after time slot, and will command prime rates.

Choose a date, and a few alternates. Once you've decided on the date you want, remember that you'll still need to be somewhat flexible. You must always have a couple of backup days set aside in case your first choice of facility is booked on a particular day. Popular reception locations often book more than a year in advance, so having a backup is especially important if you are arranging the wedding in less than six months. The same holds true if you are having the ceremony in a separate location, be it a house of worship or a park. Make sure your date is available for both your ceremony and reception sites before signing contracts for any other services. Use **Worksheet 3** to iron out the date.

The holiday weekend wedding. Holiday weekends bring up another debate altogether. Some of your guests, particularly those from out of town, will be thrilled because it will give them more time to spend with you. Others might think it inconsiderate of you to plan an event during a weekend that people typically want to spend otherwise. Remember that many holiday weekends draw peak rates for airfare and hotel accommodations, something you might want to consider if you have a lot of out-of-town guests. As the saying goes, you can't please all of the people all of the time, and someone will always have a negative opinion about your decisions. Choose the date that works for you and your families, and be understanding if a few of your guests are unable to attend.

Let people know. Once your date is finalized, spread the word so that friends and families can have it on their calendar when they are planning vacations, parties, and other events down the line, and so that those who will have to travel can have plenty of time to make arrangements. Either call people, or send informal notes, postcards, or e-mail.

Setting the time of day. It's a good idea to get the time of day nailed down early, too—you'll need to have a firm handle on this detail when you book your musicians, photographer, florist, and other service providers. Once all the pertinent contracts are signed, you'll be able to get the invitations out of the way.

Worksheet 3: Setting the Date

Starting with a few alternates, you can determine a date that will work for you by checking what days are available for the venue and/or reception hall of your choice. If you have your heart set on a particular photographer, musician, or clergyman, use the additional rows in the same manner.

POTENTIAL DATES	First choice __/__/__	Second choice __/__/__	Third choice __/__/__
Venue #1:			
Venue #2:			
Venue #3:			
Venue #4:			
Ceremony site #1:			
Ceremony site #2:			
Other:			
Other:			

Choosing the Reception Site

Finding a site for your reception may seem an overwhelming chore, but it can be quite a lot of fun to visit so many wonderful spaces. After you've set the budget, make a list of every possible location of interest, and start calling.

Be sure that the two of you are happy with the choice that you've made. Before leaving a deposit on the hall or caterer of your choice, make certain that you've answered, or at least addressed, the following questions.

- ☐ Is the date I want available?
- ☐ Are other dates or times of year more economical?
- ☐ What is the size of the room?
- ☐ What is the condition of the room?
- ☐ How far is it from the ceremony location?
- ☐ Is there a separate site fee?
- ☐ What is the maximum capacity?
- ☐ Must I guarantee a minimum number of guests?
- ☐ Is the space wheelchair-accessible?
- ☐ Is there a space for the ceremony?
- ☐ Is there an outdoor space or exceptional view?
- ☐ Is there a dance floor? Size?
- ☐ Are there other events scheduled here on the same day?
- ☐ How far in advance is it available for setup?
- ☐ Are there parking facilities? Valet parking?
- ☐ Are the rest rooms adequate?
- ☐ Is there a coat room? Attendant?
- ☐ What are the kitchen facilities?
- ☐ Does everything seem to be in good condition?
- ☐ Is there an on-site caterer? Can I use an outside caterer?
- ☐ Do you have a liquor license?
- ☐ Can I purchase my own liquor? Is there a corkage fee?
- ☐ What is the cost per person?
- ☐ Are there other fees?
- ☐ Have you worked at this location before (for off-site caterers)?

- [ ] Have you catered an event of this type and size before?
- [ ] Can I see the room set up for an event like mine?
- [ ] Are there photographs of other events I can review?
- [ ] Can I arrange a tasting to sample the menu items?
- [ ] Can I request special dishes?
- [ ] Can you handle special dietary concerns?
- [ ] Can I bring in a cake from another source?
- [ ] What staff-to-guest ratio do you recommend?
- [ ] Are gratuities included?
- [ ] Is there an escalation clause?
- [ ] What kind of deposit do you require?
- [ ] When is the balance due?
- [ ] Is there a cancellation policy?
- [ ] How many hours am I contracting for?
- [ ] Are there overtime fees?
- [ ] What kind of liability coverage do you have?
- [ ] When do you need a final head count?
- [ ] Are you responsible for renting linens, chairs, or other necessities?
- [ ] Do you coordinate the schedule with the musicians?
- [ ] Do you have any other vendors that you would recommend?
- [ ] Is there a reduced cost for children's meals? Vendors' meals?
- [ ] How will the staff be dressed?
- [ ] Do I have a choice of linens or china?
- [ ] Are there restrictions about music, dancing, or decoration?

Once your decision is made, get a written contract outlining all terms and conditions of service, including date and time of the event, fees and extra costs and deposits (including overtime, gratuities, and escalation clauses), setup times, restrictions, responsibility for cleanup, and cancellation fees.

# Worksheet 4: Booking a Reception Site

Call or visit several sites to get a sense of their services and prices. Ask for the complete price range, find out if there is a fee for the hall as well as a per-plate charge, and determine whether you will have to guarantee a certain number of guests. Ask also if the given prices include such items as the wedding cake, gratuities, centerpieces, and/or your choice of table linens. Take notes below on each site, and make comparisons before narrowing down your choices.

Site #1	Site #2
_____	_____
Prices	Prices
day _____	day _____
evening _____	evening _____
other _____	other _____
minimum/maximum _____	minimum/maximum _____
includes: _____	includes: _____
_____	_____
_____	_____
_____	_____

Site #3	Site #4
_____	_____
Prices	Prices
day _____	day _____
evening _____	evening _____
other _____	other _____
minimum/maximum _____	minimum/maximum _____
includes: _____	includes: _____
_____	_____
_____	_____
_____	_____

Choosing a Ceremony Site and an Officiant

Your wedding ceremony will be one of the most meaningful rituals in which you will participate during your life. Choosing the style and substance of your vows should be a carefully thought-out process that you and your betrothed have agreed upon. Be it a religious ceremony that reflects your spiritual beliefs or a civil ceremony performed by a legal officiant, discuss your ideas together and decide on a ceremony that resonates with both of you.

If you are planning on a civil ceremony, look for authorized officiants in your area by doing the research at the marriage license bureau of your local county clerk's office—the same place where you will get your marriage license.

If you wish to marry in a house of worship, check with the clergy immediately. In some cases, you must be a member of the congregation in order to use the facilities. In other cases, there may be certain stipulations, such as pre-marital counseling, that you will need to fulfill before being married there. You may need to provide your officiant with certain religious certificates. In addition, many houses of worship have restrictions regarding the day of the week for marriages and the type of music that is allowed, bans against photography, or even regulations about leaving flower arrangements on the altar after the ceremony is over. Secular locations often have restrictions as well. There may be decorations or customs that are forbidden, such as aisle runners or tossing birdseed or petals.

Whether you decide to get married in a house of worship, aboard a ship, or in a city park, there are a number of questions you'll need to consider. Set aside some time to sit down and talk with the priest, the rabbi, the judge, or whomever is in charge at the site of your choice, and find out what a wedding at their facility will require. Wherever you choose to wed, use the checklist below to help determine if the site will fulfill all your needs.

- [ ] Is the date I want available? If not, what are my alternatives?
- [ ] Are there any restrictions on dates or times?
- [ ] Do we have to be members of the congregation?
- [ ] Will you marry us if we are divorced, and what documentation do you require?

- [ ] Will you marry us if we are of different faiths, and are there any conditions? Will you perform the marriage with an officiant of a different faith?
- [ ] Is pre-marital counseling required?
- [ ] What are the fees?
- [ ] Are there restrictions regarding attire?
- [ ] Can we personalize our vows? Are there restrictions about readings?
- [ ] Are other weddings scheduled for the same day?
- [ ] What is the seating capacity?
- [ ] Is the site wheelchair-accessible?
- [ ] Is there a changing room for the bride?
- [ ] Are there parking facilities?
- [ ] Are photography and videography permitted? Are there any restrictions?
- [ ] Is there an organ and organist? Choir?
- [ ] Can we use our own musicians?
- [ ] Are there any restrictions on the type of music?
- [ ] Are we allowed to throw rice, birdseed, or petals?
- [ ] Are there restrictions regarding decoration?

Tips

Call several months in advance to check the requirements for your marriage license. In some states there may be a waiting period, and you will need to find out the fees, what types of identification and records you need to bring, and if blood tests are necessary.

Worksheet 5: Choosing a Ceremony Site

If you are looking for someplace special for your wedding, you'll need to plan carefully. Public parks and gardens may require special services, and particular churches may require sponsorship from a member of the congregation, or some kind of pre-marital counseling. Based on the site you choose, you may be limited in the type of officiant that can perform the ceremony. Be sure to look at practical matters as well, such as where your guests can park, what to do if it rains (if the venue is outdoors), and whether the fees include setup and cleanup. Make some calls, take notes, and compare.

Site #1	Site #2
_____	_____
Fees _____	Fees _____
Permits or other requirements _____	Permits or other requirements _____
_____	_____
_____	_____
Officiant _____	Officiant _____
Backup for rain? _____	Backup for rain? _____
Parking _____	Parking _____

Site #3	Site #4
_____	_____
Fees _____	Fees _____
Permits or other requirements _____	Permits or other requirements _____
_____	_____
_____	_____
Officiant _____	Officiant _____
Backup for rain? _____	Backup for rain? _____
Parking _____	Parking _____

The Guest List

The site and style of your wedding—along with the budget—will often hinge upon the size of your guest list. While weddings seem to bring friends and relations out of the woodwork to be added to your ever-growing guest list, you must not lose sight of the other decisions you have made. The number of people you will invite is directly related to the capacity of your ceremony and reception sites, budgetary concerns, and your personal vision about the wedding.

Ironing out your guest list can be one of the most tedious and difficult tasks involved in planning your wedding. Start your guest list immediately, and have your families do the same.

Once you've gotten a handle on how many people you'd like to invite, assess the list against your budget and decide how much you'll be able to spend per guest at the reception.

Tips

The debate about whether to invite children to a wedding is a heated one, and completely subjective. Some feel that weddings should be "adult-only" affairs, others think the joy that a crowd of giggling children adds to a celebration is priceless. Only you can determine what your personal preferences are in this matter. One compromise is to provide baby-sitters for friends with children. The children can attend the ceremony and the first hour or so of the reception, and then their sitters can take them home or to a nearby hotel.

Creating—and cutting—the guest list. Use **Worksheet 6** to estimate a preliminary guest list. Keep in mind that 20 to 25 percent of those invited will usually decline the invitation. If the list still winds up being too long, pare it down, using a set of consistently applied criteria: for example, you might eliminate anyone you haven't been in touch with for more than a year, or coworkers that you don't see outside the office. Put those guests on an alternate list, and if you find yourself able to invite them later on, as other guests decline or you find money in the budget, be prepared to send them an invitation.

Getting your guest list completed as early as possible is an absolute necessity. You'll need time to track down addresses for people who have moved, to order invitations, and to write them out. If you can get the invites out earlier, you'll be able to get responses back sooner, making it possible to invite those guests you had to cut from the first-round list.

Worksheet 6: Preliminary Guest List

Fill in the names of all those family members and friends whom you would like to invite to your wedding, and make sure you have addresses for all of them. If you come in over budget, cross off some names, and consider those guests as alternates. Have the addresses for alternates available, too, in case you're able to invite them after all. Don't forget to include guests for your single friends, who might be in a relationship by the time your wedding rolls around!

1. _____
2. _____
3. _____
4. _____
5. _____
6. _____
7. _____
8. _____
9. _____
10. _____
11. _____
12. _____
13. _____
14. _____
15. _____
16. _____
17. _____
18. _____
19. _____
20. _____
21. _____

22. _____
23. _____
24. _____
25. _____
26. _____
27. _____
28. _____
29. _____
30. _____
31. _____
32. _____
33. _____
34. _____
35. _____
36. _____
37. _____
38. _____
39. _____
40. _____
41. _____
42. _____

43. _____

44. _____

45. _____

46. _____

47. _____

48. _____

49. _____

50. _____

51. _____

52. _____

53. _____

54. _____

55. _____

56. _____

57. _____

58. _____

59. _____

60. _____

61. _____

62. _____

63. _____

64. _____

65. _____

66. _____

67. _____

68. _____

69. _____

70. _____

71. _____

72. _____

73. _____

74. _____

75. _____

76. _____

77. _____

78. _____

79. _____

80. _____

81. _____

82. _____

83. _____

84. _____

85. _____

86. _____

87. _____

88. _____

89. _____

90. _____

91. _____

92. _____

93. _____

94. _____

95. _____

96. _____

97. _____

98. _____

99. _____

100. _____

101. _____

102. _____

103. _____

104. _____

105. _____   136. _____
106. _____   137. _____
107. _____   138. _____
108. _____   139. _____
109. _____   140. _____
110. _____   141. _____
111. _____   142. _____
112. _____   143. _____
113. _____   144. _____
114. _____   145. _____
115. _____   146. _____
116. _____   147. _____
117. _____   148. _____
118. _____   149. _____
119. _____   150. _____
120. _____   151. _____
121. _____   152. _____
122. _____   153. _____
123. _____   154. _____
124. _____   155. _____
125. _____   156. _____
126. _____   157. _____
127. _____   158. _____
128. _____   159. _____
129. _____   160. _____
130. _____   161. _____
131. _____   162. _____
132. _____   163. _____
133. _____   164. _____
134. _____   165. _____
135. _____   166. _____

167. _____
168. _____
169. _____
170. _____
171. _____
172. _____
173. _____
174. _____
175. _____
176. _____
177. _____
178. _____
179. _____
180. _____
181. _____
182. _____
183. _____
184. _____
185. _____
186. _____
187. _____
188. _____
189. _____
190. _____
191. _____
192. _____
193. _____
194. _____
195. _____
196. _____
197. _____

198. _____
199. _____
200. _____
201. _____
202. _____
203. _____
204. _____
205. _____
206. _____
207. _____
208. _____
209. _____
210. _____
211. _____
212. _____
213. _____
214. _____
215. _____
216. _____
217. _____
218. _____
219. _____
220. _____
221. _____
222. _____
223. _____
224. _____
225. _____
226. _____
227. _____
228. _____

Chapter Three

The Honour of Your Presence

Once you've got the date, time, place, and style set, it is a good idea to get the ball rolling on your invitations. Although it seems like a simple process, getting your invitations in the mail, organizing your responses, keeping track of gifts, and helping friends who arrive from out of town can be some of the most time-consuming and stressful aspects of planning your wedding. So it's best to get organized early—by starting out right, you'll be able to keep the process under control right up until the week before your wedding, when you'll no doubt be calling all those people who have forgotten to respond.

The Guest List Revisited

Once you've worked out your guest list, you'll need to begin compiling your final list, including not only names but also addresses for everyone included. If you have a B-list of alternate guests, be sure to gather all the appropriate information for them as well.

Rather than a simple list, many brides find it helpful to create a file, using one 3 x 5-inch index card for each guest (or couple). You'll also need a file box with alphabetical dividers to keep the cards in order. Hand a stack to each of your parents, and have them fill out the pertinent information for each of their guests, while you do the same for your friends.

Each card should include the full name of each guest, and that guest's date if appropriate, addresses, phone numbers, and courtesy titles (Dr., Esq., Rev., etc.). Be sure to leave space for extra information—address corrections, gifts received, thank-you notes sent, and so on. You might also repeat the first letter of the last name (or one person's last name, if they are different) in the top left-hand corner for alphabetizing purposes. Once alphabetized, you're ready to get started when your invitations arrive. Be sure to remove the B-list cards, and either rubber-band them together or keep them in a different file. Use the sample card on the following page as a template.

```
C   Mr. and Mrs. John D. Connor
    219 West 91st Street
    New York, NY     10023
    (212) 555·7721
    RESPONSE: YES, two will attend
    RECEIVED: two Waterford toasting glasses 7·8·98
    THANK YOU SENT: 7·9·98
```

Tips

Some brides like to type their file cards or to create a database on a computer that includes the same information. A computerized database can make sorting the names faster and easier. But beware the old "garbage in, garbage out" rule: one little typographical error can result in an undelivered invitation or thank-you note down the line.

Out-of-town guests. If you anticipate having a number of guests travel long distances to attend your wedding, it's best to get started now on making arrangements for lodging, transportation, and other courtesies as needed. It is customary for the hosts to reserve a block of rooms at a nearby hotel. Hotels will usually provide information cards with rates and directions, which can be enclosed with the invitations. Out-of-town guests will be further discussed in chapter nine.

Guests with dates. Inviting single friends with dates is a matter of choice. As a general rule, if a single friend is engaged or in a serious relationship, his or her partner should be invited as well. Although traditional etiquette dictates that you should

The Honour of Your Presence

send a separate invitation to your friend's companion at his or her own home, it is widely accepted to send one invitation with both names to your friend's home. If there is no "significant other" but you wish to indicate that your friend can bring a date, write "and Guest" after his or her name on the inner envelope.

Choosing Your Invitations

Your wedding invitation is the first indication your guests have of the style of the wedding. Choosing an invitation that reflects that style is simple, and you have a vast expanse of invitations from which to make your selection.

A visit to a stationer, card store, or specialty paper shop will get you started. You can review books of sample invitations, discuss proper wording, look at paper samples, and see the differences between printing processes. Your invitations can be ordered through these sources, as well as through some department stores or by mail-order catalog. Consider your options for printing in relation to your budget. Engraved invitations are very elegant but also very expensive. Thermography is a less expensive option that still gives a formal, raised appearance to the type. You may even choose to make the invitations yourself using your computer and pre-packaged software and paper, or even to hire a calligrapher to produce them.

Invitations can take as little as five days and as long as four weeks to print. Make sure you order extras in case of mistakes during the addressing stage, or for last-minute additions to your guest list. Many people have their invitations addressed by a calligrapher. If you intend to do this, leave extra time for the calligrapher to do the work. It may be a good idea to ask if you can get the envelopes before the invitations in order to get started with the addressing process.

Special Inserts

There are a number of elements that can be included with the invitation, and you should make sure to have them all printed at the same time you order your invitations.

Reception card. Reception information is often indicated on the main invitation. However, some people prefer a separate enclosure on which to put the detailed information about the reception, including the time it begins and the location, using the main invitation for ceremony information only.

Choose all stationery items at the same time: invitations, reception cards, pew cards, directions or maps, response cards, thank-you notes, wedding announcements (only for people who were not invited to the wedding), and all necessary envelopes, programs, place cards, personalized matches and napkins, and at-home cards (indicating your new address after the wedding and the date you will be moving). Check postal restrictions regarding envelope size, especially for small RSVP cards.

Pew card. For select guests who will be escorted to reserved seating in one of the first few rows, a pew card should be inserted. The guest will hand the pew card to the usher upon arriving at the ceremony to alert him to special seating arrangements. This is also known as a "within the ribbon" card.

Maps and directions. Guests may need instructions about getting to the ceremony or traveling between the ceremony and the reception, so a specific insert for this information is frequently included.

Hotel information. For out-of-town guests who need overnight accommodations, you should include the names, addresses, and telephone numbers of several local hotels or inns. If you have arranged a group rate at a specific place, include that information as well.

RSVP card. Most wedding invitations include a pre-printed card with a self-addressed stamped envelope. To respond to the invitation, the guest simply writes in his or her name and the number of people attending. If the caterer requires an advance count on the guests' selections for dinner, this is where the choices will be printed; guests merely check off their preference.

Wording

An informal invitation can use any wording you choose as long as it conveys clearly the basic information to the guest: who, when, where, what type, and how to respond.

Most wedding invitations use a classic style of wording, however. Names are written out in full and the title is the only thing that is abbreviated. Traditionally, "honour" and "favour" use the anglicized spelling. Dates and times are also spelled out rather than numeralized. Adding the year is optional, as is adding the city, although it is a good idea to clarify the exact location unless all the guests are from the same local area. Traditional wordings follow, but there are infinite variations on these samples, and if you wish, you can use an entirely nontraditional wording.

A professional stationer can help you determine the best wording for your invitation. Carefully write out your preferred wording for the invitation, enclosures, and the return envelopes, and have more than one person check them for errors. If it varies at all from traditional wording, make a notation to print as written, or the stationer may change it to conform to custom without consulting you. Use **Worksheet 7** to determine your stationery needs and finalize your invitation wording.

When the invitations arrive from the stationer, proofread them carefully. Mail invitations approximately four to six weeks prior to the wedding, giving guests up to two weeks before the wedding to respond. The caterer will probably want a final guest count about one week before the wedding, so leave yourself some time to call guests in case you do not receive their response cards. For overseas guests, consider sending invitations out eight weeks in advance.

When the bride's parents host.

Mr. and Mrs. Matthew Loden
request the honour of your presence
at the marriage of their daughter
Eliza Brook
to
Mr. Anthony Michael Ritchard
on Saturday, the fifth of June
Two thousand and one
at five o'clock in the evening
The Picnic House
Prospect Park West
Lynbrook, New York

Reception and dinner immediately following

When the bride's parents host, but wish to include the groom's parents.

Mr. and Mrs. Matthew Loden

request the honour of your presence

at the marriage of their daughter

Eliza Brook

to

Anthony Michael Ritchard

son of

Mr. and Mrs. Jerome Ritchard

etc.

When divorced parents cohost.

Mrs. Beatrice Loden

and

Mr. Matthew Loden

request the honour of your presence

at the marriage of their daughter

Eliza Brook

etc.

When divorced and remarried parents cohost.

Dr. and Mrs. John Lane Thornbury

and

Mr. Matthew Loden

request the honour of your presence

at the marriage of

Eliza Brook

etc.

When the groom's parents host.

Mr. and Mrs. Jerome Ritchard

request the honour of your presence

at the marriage of

Miss Eliza Brook Loden

to their son

Anthony Michael Ritchard

etc.

The Honour of Your Presence

When the bride's and groom's parents cohost.

Mr. and Mrs. Matthew Loden

and

Mr. and Mrs. Jerome Ritchard

request the honour of your presence

at the marriage of

Eliza Brook Loden

and

Anthony Michael Ritchard

etc.

When the bride and groom host.

The honour of your presence is requested

at the marriage of

Eliza Brook Loden

to

Anthony Michael Ritchard

etc.

Worksheet 7: Ordering Your Invitations

Use this worksheet to indicate what supplies you'll need from your stationer. Order enough invitations to cover your entire guest list, along with extras for any addressing errors, for additional guests, and for keepsakes. Remember your budget!

Total number of invitations _____

Enclosures

    reception cards

    response cards

    pew cards

    directions

    hotel cards

    other: _____

Other items

    thank-you cards

    announcements

    napkins

    matchbooks

    other: _____

Desired Wording

Invitation

_____

_____

_____

_____

_____

_____

_____

_____

_____

_____

The Honour of Your Presence

_____

_____

_____

_____

_____

_____

_____

Reception card

_____

_____

_____

_____

_____

Response card

_____

_____

_____

_____

_____

Return address (for envelopes)

_____

_____

_____

_____

_____

Addressing and Mailing

Addressing and mailing envelopes is a time-consuming and detailed job. However, it is one of those tasks that can be easily delegated or split among a few people. Some couples hire professional calligraphers to address their envelopes, others do them themselves, and still others recruit their bridesmaids, ushers, and/or friends or family members to pitch in, breaking the list down into batches of twenty or so envelopes each.

When all the components are together, take a sample to the post office and have it weighed so that you can then purchase the correct postage for the invitations. Don't forget to get stamps for your response envelopes.

Addressing the envelopes. Your invitations will include a glued outer envelope and an unsealed envelope inside. For a formal invitation, both envelopes should be hand-addressed in black ink.

The outer envelope includes the complete names and address of your invited guests (not including children or a guest's date). The inner envelope includes your guests' names, including those of any children or dates who are invited with them. There are a few general rules to keep in mind when addressing both envelopes.

+ The outer envelope includes the complete names of your guests, followed by their address.
+ The inner envelope includes only the title and last name of each guest.
+ The names of invited children should not appear on the outer envelope. Their names should follow their parents' names on a separate line on the inner envelope only.
+ Names and addresses, except for titles (Dr., Mr., Mrs., Ms.), should not be abbreviated on either envelope.
+ On both envelopes, married couples with different last names and couples living together receive one invitation with both names written on separate lines.
+ Couples with distinctive courtesy titles may also require separate lines.
+ If a married female uses a distinctive title, such as Dr., her name should appear before her husband's.
+ If a friend is being invited with a date whose name you don't know, only your friend's name should appear on the outer envelope. On the inner envelope, the friend's name should be followed by "and Guest."

The table below provides basic rules of thumb for writing out the names of your guests on your invitations.

	Outer envelope	Inner envelope
Married couple with same last name	Mr. and Mrs. Jonathan Smith 519 Widgeon Way Spring Lake, New Jersey 10349	Mr. and Mrs. Smith
Married couple with different last names, or couple living together	Ms. Bernadette Shea Mr. Jason Strickland 123 Chatham Road Hyannis, Massachusetts 02601	Ms. Shea and Mr. Strickland
Single guest with a date	Mr. Michael Morrisey 315 Newport Avenue Berkeley, California 91402	Mr. Morrisey and Guest
Children under sixteen, invited with their parents	Mr. and Mrs. Edward Taylor 3100 Deakin Street Chicago, Illinois 60611	Mr. and Mrs. Taylor Katie and Max
Married couple in which woman holds a special title	Dr. Mary Cassidy Mr. Thomas Cassidy 557 York Avenue Toronto, Ontario Canada B312LX	Dr. Cassidy and Mr. Cassidy
Married couple in which man holds a special title	Captain Daniel Paine Mrs. Anne Paine 104 South Chestnut Avenue Sioux City, Iowa 55019	Captain and Mrs Paine

Keep in mind the following rules of thumb as well.

- Single women—even children—should always be addressed as Ms. or Miss.
- A widow should be addressed by her husband's name: Mrs. Jonathan Smith.
- A divorced woman should be addressed by her own first name (not her ex-husband's), and the last name that she uses: Mrs. Evelyn Braynor or Ms. Evelyn Stockton.
- For couples invited together who do not live together, separate invitations should be sent if possible.
- Young people over sixteen years of age who live with their parents should receive a separate invitation.

Keeping Track of Responses

As your guests respond, either in person or by phone, mail, or returning the response card, mark their responses on their file card. Immediately move the "No" responses into a separate pile or section, and if appropriate, take each "No" response as an opportunity to invite an additional guest from the B-list. As you invite alternates, be sure to move their cards out of the B-list and into the regular file, then make a note of the date that the invitation was sent out, so that you can allow them a bit more time to respond.

Table Arrangements

Once all your responses are in, you'll need to sit down and iron out your floor plan. The beauty of the file-card system is that it will allow you to easily shuffle your guests around as you create table arrangements for your reception.

Seating your guests. Find out from your caterer how many guests can be seated comfortably at each table. Then begin assembling cards for your "Yes" respondents into table groups, clipping sets of cards with a paper clip.

Once you've gotten your tables settled, you will have to arrange them on a floor plan. Keep in mind where the band will be set up, how you want the bridal party seated, and the location and size of the dance floor. Try to seat older guests, who might be bothered by loud music, away from the band or the deejay's amplifiers.

The Honour of Your Presence

Occasionally, in the excitement to send back an invitation, a guest may actually forget to write in his or her name, and you are left wondering who it is who has responded. Here's a trick to avoid confusion: when you write up your guest list, assign a number for every invitation that will be sent. Write that number in an inconspicuous place on the back of the RSVP card. If it is returned unsigned, you can look up, say, number 117 on your guest list and instantly know that Aunt Carol and Uncle Gene will be in attendance!

Seating the bridal party. Tradition dictates that the bride and groom sit with their bridesmaids and ushers at a long formal table set apart from other guests. Formally called a dais, this "head table" is often set upon a raised platform, with the wedding party situated only on one side so that they can look out over the reception. The bride and groom are seated at the center of the table, with the best man to the bride's right and the maid of honor to the groom's left. The other attendants are positioned in an alternating male-female pattern radiating out to the ends of the table.

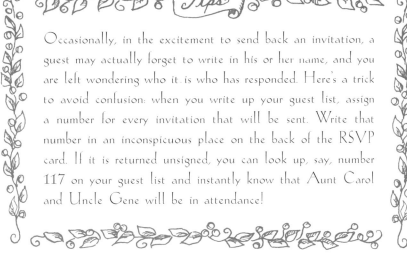

The dais idea is used because it lends a formal air to the reception, and allows other guests to gaze upon the guests of honor while giving the bride and groom a bird's-eye view of the goings-on at their party. However, many couples find the dais uncomfortable and impractical. Seated only on one side of the table, the wedding party will find it difficult to relax in conversation with one another, and many people dislike the idea of being placed so prominently on display. Another potential problem with the dais is that attendants are not able to sit with their dates.

One option is for the bride and groom to sit with the best man and maid of honor and their dates, or to sit with their parents. A charming new trend seats the bride and groom alone at a sweethearts' table while their attendants sit with their dates at tables set up near the newlyweds.

Seating your parents and families. If they are not sitting with you, your parents should be seated near the front of the room, either at separate "bride's side" and "groom's side" tables or together with the officiant and other honored guests. However, you can break down your family tables any way you like, depending on the size of your families, your tables, and the total number of guests.

Place cards. Once you've finalized your floor plan, you can either order or write up place cards that will indicate at what table guests are seated. Get these cards to the reception site, along with the final head count, a few days before the wedding, and note any specific instructions regarding their placement.

Alternatively, you might consider creating a seating list, and having the reception hall post several attendants at the door who can then escort guests to their tables as they arrive.

Chapter Four

Dressing for the Occasion

Rarely will you put so much thought into your attire as you will for your wedding day. Both bride and groom will be the center of attention, and their attire, along with that of their attendants, will very much set the mood for the event, be it traditional or modern, formal or casual.

Bridal Basics

For many brides, choosing a gown and headpiece is the most important step in preparing for the wedding. And with the variety of styles, prices, and even colors to choose from, the process can be overwhelming but ultimately satisfying.

Make an appointment at a bridal boutique, and bring only one person along with you. Traditional bridal gowns can take up to six months from the time you order to be ready, so if you choose to go that route, start shopping early. Bring pictures of the types of gowns you like, and be honest about your price range. If you already have certain accessories that you intend to wear—a pearl necklace or your mother's tiara—bring them along when you shop for your dress. Be prepared to explain the style and formality of your wedding, and let the salesperson know your wedding date.

When you have chosen a gown, the salesperson will take your measurements to send to the manufacturer and the gown will be made to order. However, most brides still need one or two rounds of alterations to get the dress to the perfect fit. Alteration fees are rarely included in the price of a wedding gown, so find out in advance what you will be charged for the fittings and have all fees, conditions, and policies outlined in your order.

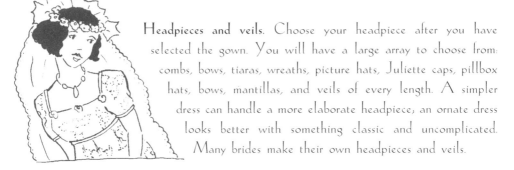

Headpieces and veils. Choose your headpiece after you have selected the gown. You will have a large array to choose from: combs, bows, tiaras, wreaths, picture hats, Juliette caps, pillbox hats, bows, mantillas, and veils of every length. A simpler dress can handle a more elaborate headpiece; an ornate dress looks better with something classic and uncomplicated. Many brides make their own headpieces and veils.

Shoes. You'll be on your feet all day long—dancing, posing for photos, and mingling with friends and family. Make sure that your shoes have a sturdy heel and a comfortable fit, and consider lining them with cushioned insoles. Do break them in before your wedding—wear them around the house (on carpeting, where they won't get scuffed) to soften them up—and take a little sandpaper to the soles to improve traction and prevent any slipups on your wedding day. If you are having an outdoor wedding, remember that spiky heels will sink right into the ground.

Underpinnings. You'll undoubtedly need a special bra to wear under your dress, especially if it has an off-the-shoulder sleeve or a low back. Try on as many as possible and hold the receipts, in case you find out at your fitting that what you bought won't work. Depending on your dress, you might find you'll need a petticoat as well.

When you make your decision about a gown, ask the salesperson to bring you several petticoats of varying stiffness, and decide which one you like best under your gown. Then find out where you can buy one just like it.

Tips

Purchase your wedding shoes and undergarments before you go in for your first fitting. Wearing shoes and petticoats will affect the length of the dress, and wearing different ones to the fitting can result in a hemline that is a bit too long or short when you walk down the aisle.

Dressing for the Occasion

Find stockings that fit well and complement the color of your dress. Consider both pantyhose and thigh-high stockings (which are much cooler in the summertime), but make sure you have a good garter belt to hold up the latter.

Other accessories. You can also add gloves, a purse, jewelry, and a wrap to complete your ensemble. Don't go overboard—there's no sense in carrying a wrap in the summertime, and if your dress has long sleeves, gloves are inappropriate. Choose your jewelry carefully, and consider borrowing pieces from friends and relatives. Your purse should be simple and small, although many brides require a larger bag to carry envelopes and small gifts that they receive on their wedding day.

Menswear

The bride and groom will decide on the level of formality of men's clothing as well. Traditionally, the tuxedo or dinner jacket is worn only after 6 P.M., but these days many men wear tuxedos during their daytime weddings. Following strict rules of etiquette, a man will wear a cutaway coat, striped trousers, and an ascot during the day. A white tie and tails are reserved for a very formal evening celebration. A dark suit is perfect for an informal wedding, and a blazer and trousers can be worn to a more casual affair.

Although the bride more often than not steals the show in terms of fashion, many grooms put a good deal of thought into what they will wear on their wedding day. The groom's attire need not exactly match that of his attendants. Some simply choose to purchase rather than rent tuxedos, while others have ties, vests, and/or cummerbunds specially made from particular fabrics, such as family tartans or fraternity colors. Members of the military might choose to be married in their dress uniform, and some men's wardrobes might include ethnic elements, such as a kilt.

The groomsmen and the fathers take their cue from the groom, and usually wear attire to match his. However, like any custom, this tradition can be altered to suit your personal style. The groom and his attendants can rent their attire, and should make their selections and be measured approximately three months before the wedding. They will also have to make decisions about shirts, ties, vests or cummerbunds, and other accessories.

Worksheet 8: Bride's & Groom's Wedding Attire Checklist

Use this worksheet as a checklist to prepare for all the necessities of your wedding day attire. The first column indicates that you've purchased—or borrowed, or inherited, or already have—the item. Use the second column as a last-minute checklist to ensure that everything is ready—and, if necessary, packed—the day before your wedding.

Bride's Attire	Purchased	Packed
Gown	☐	☐
Slip/petticoat	☐	☐
Bra and panties	☐	☐
Stockings (two pairs)	☐	☐
Other undergarment	☐	☐
Earrings	☐	☐
Necklace	☐	☐
Other jewelry	☐	☐
Gloves	☐	☐
Purse	☐	☐
Headpiece and veil	☐	☐
Shoes	☐	☐
Wrap or shawl	☐	☐
Makeup	☐	☐
Nail polish	☐	☐
Hair products	☐	☐
Other items:		
_____	☐	☐
_____	☐	☐

Groom's Attire	Purchased	Packed
Jacket	☐	☐
Trousers	☐	☐
Shirt	☐	☐
Collar	☐	☐
Tie	☐	☐
Vest/cummerbund	☐	☐
Cufflinks, studs, tie clip	☐	☐
Shoes	☐	☐
Socks	☐	☐
Spats	☐	☐
Razor and toiletries	☐	☐
Other items:		
_____	☐	☐
_____	☐	☐

Bridesmaids' Dresses

When selecting your attendants' gowns, keep their figure types in mind and try to choose a style that will be flattering on everyone. Show concern for your attendants' feelings, and choose something that they like and can afford. Your maid of honor can wear either the same gown as your other attendants or a different but complementary one. Young girls can wear a dress similar to that of the bridesmaids, or a white dress, and often they wear a crown of flowers. Junior bridesmaids usually wear a similar but age-appropriate version of the bridesmaids' gowns.

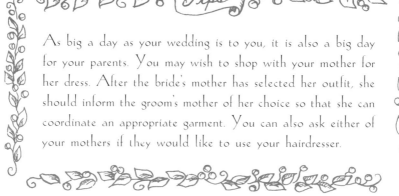

As big a day as your wedding is to you, it is also a big day for your parents. You may wish to shop with your mother for her dress. After the bride's mother has selected her outfit, she should inform the groom's mother of her choice so that she can coordinate an appropriate garment. You can also ask either of your mothers if they would like to use your hairdresser.

Wedding Day Beauty

If you choose to have a professional handle your hair and/or makeup, make arrangements early on and prepare a test-run for both shortly before your wedding. Bring your headpiece along, and perhaps a photo or drawing of the top of your dress, to help your hairdresser envision the neckline. If you have makeup colors that you prefer, be vocal about it, or even bring your own makeup along with you. Make an appointment for a manicure as well—a lot of people will be staring at your hands on your wedding day.

Ask your bridesmaids if they would like to have any of these services performed as well. A "morning of beauty," including facials, manicures, and makeovers, is a fun and relaxing start to your wedding day. Make all necessary appointments, and note them in **Worksheet 9**.

Worksheet 9: Hair & Makeup Appointments

If you arrange hair, makeup, and manicure appointments for yourself, your mother, and/or your bridesmaids, keep track of dates and times here.

Hair

Hairdresser name _____

Phone _____

Salon _____

Fee _____

Arrives home/hotel _____

Appointments

Time _____ Name _____

Time _____ Name _____

Time _____ Name _____

Time _____ Name _____

Time _____ Name _____

Time _____ Name _____

Time _____ Name _____

Time _____ Name _____

Time _____ Name _____

Time _____ Name _____

Time _____ Name _____

Time _____ Name _____

Time _____ Name _____

Makeup

Stylist name _____

Phone _____

Salon _____

Fee _____

Arrives home/hotel _____

Appointments

Time _____ Name _____

Time _____ Name _____

Time _____ Name _____

Time _____ Name _____

Time _____ Name _____

Time _____ Name _____

Time _____ Name _____

Time _____ Name _____

Time _____ Name _____

Time _____ Name _____

Time _____ Name _____

Time _____ Name _____

Time _____ Name _____

Nails

Manicures can be taken care of a day or two before the wedding, and—unless you and your bridesmaids will be scheduling a "day of beauty" the morning of the wedding—you should only have to worry about scheduling one for yourself. Make note of the date and time here.

Manicurist name _____

Phone _____

Salon _____

Fee _____

Chapter Five

Planning Your Wedding Ceremony

Have you always dreamed of a religious service steeped in tradition, or do you want to write your own vows? Will there be any special readings or musical pieces? Are there any family traditions or cultural elements—such as

jumping the broom—that you want to include? Exchanging your vows is the central point in this celebration, and the promise that you make to each other, in front of all your loved ones, is the most important part of the day. All the details of your ceremony can be worked out in **Worksheet 10.**

Personalize Your Ceremony

People often neglect to put the kind of thought into their ceremony that will make it truly their own, concentrating their efforts instead on the reception. When the time comes to plan your ceremony, seize it as an opportunity to make a statement about your life together.

Readings. Wedding ceremonies often include readings as a matter of course. Take this as an opportunity to express yourself and your relationship to all the people you have chosen to be your witnesses. Check with the officiant before making any decisions, are there any restrictions on what can be read? Then get to researching, and find that special bit of prose or poetry that speaks to both of you. Consider biblical passages, classic poetry and prose, or even an original piece written by you or someone close to you.

Music for your ceremony. Whether it is "Ave Maria," "Grow Old Along with Me," or "Sunrise, Sunset," music adds a lovely interlude to your service. Choose carefully the music for both the processional and the recessional, and perhaps a song or

two that can be sung at various moments during the ceremony. If you have a friend or relative who is musically talented, ask if he or she would be interested in taking part in your ceremony.

Work out the music with both officiant (again, remember to ask about restrictions) and musicians well in advance. You can plan out the music with the parts of your ceremony in **Worksheet 10**.

Personal vows. Traditional vows have been around for centuries because they sum up the whole of married life in a rather elegant way. You can make these vows more personal by memorizing them rather than repeating them after the officiant or simply saying "I do." As an alternative, consider opting for nontraditional vows, or—even more personal—try writing them yourselves. You can do this together or surprise one another at the ceremony with your own unique and special promise of love.

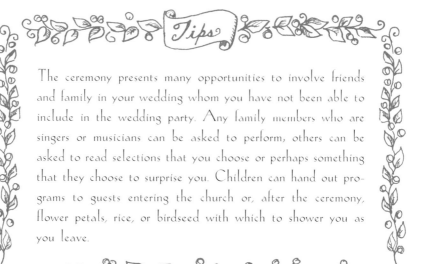

Tips

The ceremony presents many opportunities to involve friends and family in your wedding whom you have not been able to include in the wedding party. Any family members who are singers or musicians can be asked to perform, others can be asked to read selections that you choose or perhaps something that they choose to surprise you. Children can hand out programs to guests entering the church or, after the ceremony, flower petals, rice, or birdseed with which to shower you as you leave.

The Processional

Different cultures have different traditions concerning the processional. In many Christian services, the bride's mother is seated by an usher after all the other guests have been seated, and just before the processional starts. The priest or minister waits at the altar with the best man and the groom. In a Jewish wedding, it is customary for the bride and groom to be escorted down the aisle by both sets of parents, and the rabbi and cantor may either wait at the chuppah (the canopy under which a Jewish wedding ceremony takes place) or lead the processional.

Ushers and bridesmaids can walk in pairs or in single file. You may also incorporate your grandparents and other close relatives into the processional. However you decide to enter and leave the ceremony, be sure to work it out well in advance of the rehearsal, so that everyone knows what they'll be doing the day of your wedding.

Receiving Your Guests

Many couples employ a receiving line after the ceremony, seizing it as their first opportunity to greet their guests as husband and wife. You may find this is the only chance you will have to spend a few moments with each and every person, as you soon may be swept up in the festivities and not be able to take the time to visit every table. The receiving line allows you at least a moment to accept everyone's good wishes and thank them for sharing your special day.

Traditionally, the bride's mother is the first person in the receiving line, followed by the groom's mother, the bride and groom, the honor attendants, and the bridesmaids. The fathers and groomsmen are expected to mingle with the guests. As with every other aspect of wedding planning, the old rules are valid only if they work for your situation, and you should feel free to create the receiving line that you want— or even skip it altogether.

Other Details

In addition to music and readings, attention to detail at the ceremony can give a special touch to your wedding. The following are great ways to involve family or children who have not been included in the wedding party.

Programs. Many couples create wedding programs that are distributed to their guests as they are being seated for the service. The program lists the names and relationships of all members of the wedding party, the schedule for the ceremony, musical selections, readings, acknowledgments, special messages, and perhaps even your vows. This can be done as formally as you like, printed by a professional printer and bound with ribbon. Or it can be a simple list of thank-yous to everyone who took part, printed on your computer and rolled up scroll-style.

The big send-off. Though tradition dictates that rice be thrown at the couple as they leave the ceremony location, it has become widely known that this practice is harmful to birds and small animals, who may eat the uncooked rice and have it expand in their stomachs. Instead post a chosen child or friend at the door offering some alternative: birdseed, rose petals, confetti, or bubbles. Some couples have chosen to skip the shower and release balloons, butterflies, or doves after their ceremony.

Tips

Remember, if you are planning to have any part of your wedding outdoors, devise a backup plan in case of inclement weather, such as an indoor space that will accommodate your guests or a tent set up to shield the party from the elements.

Worksheet 10: Planning Your Ceremony

Once you've chosen the place, you'll need to settle the details. Keep track of all the important information here. Be sure to finalize the order for the processional, recessional, and receiving line before the rehearsal.

Site _____

Address _____

Contact person _____

Telephone _____

Reserved date _____

Contract date _____

Time _____ to _____

Deposit _____ Balance due _____

Time(s) for wedding party to arrive

   Groom and ushers _____

   Bride and bridesmaids _____

Pre-marital counseling required?___ by (date) _____

Counseling information _____

_____

Officiant _____

Telephone _____

Rings ordered/purchased _____

Programs printed _____

Marriage license _____

Accessories (chuppah, goblet, aisle runner, candelabra)

_____

_____

_____

Pew cards _____
_____
_____
_____

Processional order

1. _____
2. _____
3. _____
4. _____
5. _____
6. _____
7. _____
8. _____
9. _____
10. _____
11. _____
12. _____
13. _____
14. _____
15. _____
16. _____

Readings

1. _____ Read by _____
3. _____ Read by _____
2. _____ Read by _____
4. _____ Read by _____

Recessional order

1. _____
2. _____
3. _____

4. _____

5. _____

6. _____

7. _____

8. _____

9. _____

10. _____

Musicians and singers _____

_____

_____

_____

Phone _____

Fee _____

Prelude _____

Solo or choral piece _____

Processional _____

Bride's procession _____

Solo or hymn _____

Other _____

_____

Recessional _____

Postlude _____

_____

Receiving line order

1. _____

2. _____

3. _____

4. _____

5. _____

6. _____

Chapter Six
Planning Your Reception

You'll need to do much of the planning for your reception far in advance so that you are sure to be set with a caterer, a baker, musicians, and other service providers. The planning involves not only food, drink, and entertainment but also choosing which traditions you wish to continue and which new ones you want to start.

Food and Drink

Depending on the type of meal you plan, your catering bill, including bar tab, can add up to 50 percent of your total fees, or more! You may have to juggle the number of people you wish to invite with the type of meal you will serve in order to stay on budget. Remember that tradition states that the only "must haves" for a wedding reception are champagne and cake. However, if you have your reception at a traditional mealtime, be assured that guests will arrive expecting to be fed. If you plan anything other than a traditional meal, it is best to indicate the type of reception on the invitation.

In-house caterers. Many reception halls have in-house caterers and do not allow the use of outside caterers. You might be faced with very few options for cutting back on the catering budget—you may even have to guarantee a minimum number of guests. On the other hand, such sites offer an all-inclusive package, so you won't have to pay rental fees for tables, chairs, linens, and dishes, and they will have a fully stocked bar so you won't have to order anything special for your event; they may also offer more flexibility in terms of extra setup time and delivery of flowers.

Choosing a caterer. If you have chosen a location that is a site rental only, you may now be faced with finding an independent caterer. Some of these sites will already have a list of approved caterers for you to choose from. If you have no such restrictions, finding a caterer is a matter of using all your resources. Ask the hall manager for recommendations, talk to friends, and consult local directories, wedding magazines, and the yellow pages. You can also check in at your favorite restaurants and see if they cater parties.

As with the reception site, your first job is to telephone any caterer you are interested in and interview them on the phone (use **Worksheet 11**). As their first step, most caterers will send you some sample menus and a rough estimate of costs for the type of affair you wish to have. When you have narrowed the field down to two or three, try to visit them in person.

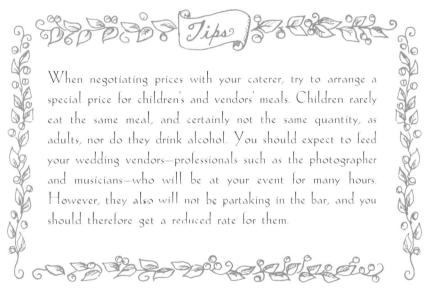

Tips

When negotiating prices with your caterer, try to arrange a special price for children's and vendors' meals. Children rarely eat the same meal, and certainly not the same quantity, as adults, nor do they drink alcohol. You should expect to feed your wedding vendors—professionals such as the photographer and musicians—who will be at your event for many hours. However, they also will not be partaking in the bar, and you should therefore get a reduced rate for them.

The icing on the cake. Some caterers include a wedding cake as part of their service. Others will agree to let you bring in a cake from an outside source. Whether you have your heart set on a confection created by a specialty baker or you have a best friend who is a talented amateur and has offered her services, your wedding cake is the crowning glory of your reception. Often on display for much of the celebration, the towering tiers or staggered layers of your cake may be either the only dessert served at your reception or the grand finale to a spectacular Viennese table—or anything in between.

Today's brides and grooms do not feel compelled to order the traditional white cake with white frosting. Wedding cakes come in all shapes, sizes, and flavors. Chocolate, carrot, almond, lemon poppy seed, and banana cakes are all making appearances at weddings. Many couples are opting for cheesecake, a different flavor for each tier of the wedding cake. Other options include butter cake, sponge cake, genoise, dacquoise, or chiffon. Fillings are just as varied, from frosting to mousse to ganache to fruit purées to pralines to cream fillings. And the icing on the cake? Well, you have several choices.

✥   **Buttercream.** Probably the tastiest choice, buttercream has a smooth consistency that melts in your mouth (and in your hand!). For the best flavor, it should be made with real butter—not margarine or vegetable shortening—although you won't get a pure white color because of this.

✥   **Royal icing.** Made of sugar and egg whites, this icing dries to a hard consistency. It is generally used to pipe decorations such as latticework, beading, and stringwork onto a frosted cake, but is sometimes smoothed over another covering to add a crunchy texture and a smooth finish.

✥   **Marzipan.** This sugary almond paste is a classic for either covering cakes or molding decorative flowers or shapes. It dries out when exposed to the elements, so it must be kept well covered.

✥   **Fondant.** Rolled fondant creates a perfectly smooth, matte surface ready for embellishment. It also helps seal in the freshness of a cake for several days. It is very sweet and chewy. On its own, the taste may be a disappointment, but fondant can cover another frosting, such as buttercream, and its perfect even texture creates the porcelain look that is often coveted on a cake. Fondant cannot be refrigerated.

✥   **Whipped cream.** Although it's a delicious covering for your cake, it is also very delicate and temperamental. It will need to stay refrigerated, and won't tolerate the addition of heavy flourishes.

Wedding cakes can be decorated in any number of ways as well, from traditional to contemporary in appearance. Some bakers will try to match your cake to the style of your wedding—a black and white cake for an Art Deco theme, a cake covered

Planning Your Reception

in chocolate and decorated with green, orange, and yellow leaves for an autumn wedding, or royal icing piped over the cake to match a swatch of lace from your wedding gown. Flowers can be formed from chocolate, pastillage (a form of rolled fondant), marzipan, or royal icing, or real blossoms grown without the use of insecticides can adorn the tiers of your cake. Petals can be pressed into the icing to match the handmade petal paper used for your invitations. The wedding baker is a true artist, and will have many ideas to help you personalize your cake.

To find a baker, check first with your caterer for recommendations, as well as with friends and family. Be sure that you will be able to see and also taste samples of the baker's work, and check for added costs for delivery of the cake.

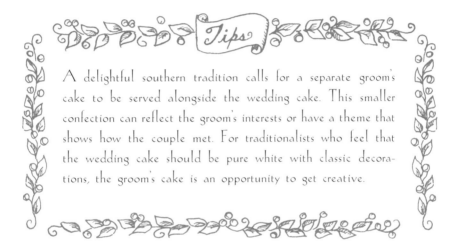

Tips

A delightful southern tradition calls for a separate groom's cake to be served alongside the wedding cake. This smaller confection can reflect the groom's interests or have a theme that shows how the couple met. For traditionalists who feel that the wedding cake should be pure white with classic decorations, the groom's cake is an opportunity to get creative.

Drinking and being merry. A catering hall or ballroom facility will be able to provide you with a complete beverage package—champagne, wine, beer, fully stocked bar, coffee, tea, and soft drinks—or any part thereof that you desire for your reception. You

may have the option to choose between an open bar for a flat fee, or a per-drink price. Look carefully at the fees and try to gauge your best option based on what you know of your guests' habits. Some caterers might offer you a discount if you serve only wine and beer, others will charge the same regardless of what you serve.

If you are using an independent caterer who does not possess a liquor license, you will be required to purchase the liquor yourself. To estimate how much your guests will consume, you can use the general formula of two drinks in the first hour and one drink every hour thereafter per guest.

Although it has become an accepted practice in certain areas, a cash bar is still considered an unsatisfactory option in most parts of the country. Some people consider it in poor taste to require guests to purchase any part of their meal, and feel it would be better to offer fewer choices—wine and beer, a champagne toast, or cocktails only while hors d'oeuvres are served—and still stay within your budget. Some couples decide not to serve spirits of any sort at their wedding. Regardless of your position on liquor, serve your guests water, soft drinks, and coffee or tea as part of the meal.

Tips

As the host of a party at which alcohol is served, when it comes to drinking and driving you are responsible for the safety of your guests as well as the community in which you are hosting. Encourage your guests to designate drivers who will abstain from drinking during the course of the festivities. Enlist the aid of others to offer a ride home to someone who has been drinking, and keep a list of local taxi services handy.

Planning Your Reception

Worksheet 11: Reception Site & Catering Checklist

Use this worksheet to keep track of details involving food and drink for your reception. Note who is responsible for each aspect, and the costs involved, as well as any and all other information you find necessary.

	Reception hall	*Caterer*
Name		
Address		
Telephone		
Banquet manager		
Reserved date		
Contract date		
Time _____ to _____		

	Reception hall	*Caterer*
Deposit		
Balance due		
Final guest count due		
MENU		
Cocktail hour		
Dinner		

	Reception hall	Caterer
Dessert		
Cake		
Beverages		
Place cards		
Favors		
Toasting glasses		
Cake knife		
Rentals needed		

Reception Music

Depending on the style of your reception, you may want anything from a classic orchestra to a rock-and-roll band to entertain your guests. Generally speaking, the size of the band should mirror the size of the hall and the number of guests. Many couples, for space or budgetary reasons, opt for a disk jockey, which costs less and can offer a greater variety of music.

Although reviewing tapes is a good way to narrow down the field, it is important to see the music professional in action at an event. And when it's time to sign the contract, be certain of who and what you are contracting for—it should, for instance, guarantee that the bandleader or lead singer whose talents sold you on their service will be the same person performing at your wedding.

Agree beforehand about the number of hours musicians will be expected to perform, what the overtime fees are, and how many breaks they will have and for how long. Let them know how you expect them to dress, the songs that you definitely want them to play (and when), and those, too, that you definitely want them to avoid. Find out if they are already familiar with the type of music you want to hear, and be prepared to provide sheet music if you wish them to learn a new song for your wedding. Disk jockeys have their own styles as well, so be certain you are in sync in terms of how much interaction there will be.

Tips

Guests will typically approach the band or deejay with requests. Do let the emcee know if there are songs that you both can't stand ("No 'Macarena'!"), and if any or all requests from guests are welcome. Discuss whether you would welcome guests who would like to give toasts from the stage, and if any musicians or singers in the crowd may perform at the reception.

Running the Party

The bandleader or deejay typically serves as master of ceremonies, or emcee, at a wedding reception, and he or she should be well aware of the way you want the party to be run. Devise a clear outline of the evening for the band to follow, including any specific instructions and a list of events you'd like to include, such as a bouquet toss or a special dance for the bride and her father. Talk to the emcee about music to accompany such festivities, and make sure you see eye-to-eye with him or her on the style of the party.

There are a number of activities that traditionally happen during the reception. Let your emcee know how you feel about certain activities, and be clear on how you want them handled. Provide him or her with names as needed! Use **Worksheet 12** to work up an outline for your reception.

Introduction of the bridal party. At many weddings, the bridal party, along with the bride's and groom's parents, are formally introduced to a room of cheering guests. They enter the room as their names are called and form a circle around the dance floor to surround the bride and groom.

First dance. The newlyweds are offered the opportunity to have one dance all to themselves, and will choose a song that has special meaning to them. The first dance may come before the best man's toast or follow it directly. It can also come between the times when the first and main courses are served.

Toasts. The best man's toast usually starts off the festivities at the reception. Often, the groom will then toast his bride, their parents, and even their guests. The bride may also make a toast if she chooses. Anyone else wishing to make a toast may do so at any time during the celebration, provided it is agreed upon beforehand with the emcee. The best toasts are positive statements of affection for the person or people being toasted. They should be short and personal, but not embarrassing.

Father/daughter dance. The bride and her father take a poignant spin around the dance floor, often joined by the groom dancing with the bride's mother, according to traditional etiquette, or his own mother.

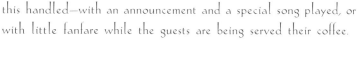

Bouquet toss. Usually near the end of the festivities, all the single women are asked to line up. The bride turns her back to them and tosses her bouquet over her shoulder. Tradition states that the woman who catches the bouquet will be the next to marry.

Garter toss. The groom removes the bride's garter from her leg and tosses it to the single men in the same fashion as the bouquet toss.

Elimination dance. This is a fairly recent addition to reception festivities. All couples are invited to join the bride and groom on the dance floor for a slow dance. As the music progresses, the bandleader "eliminates" couples by asking anyone who has been married for less than a certain amount of time to step out—less than one day eliminates the bridal couple first, a month or a year eliminates other newlyweds, five years, ten years, and so on thins the crowd even more—until finally you reach one couple who may have been married for twenty-five years, fifty years, or more. The last couple dancing "wins" and is often given a token gift, perhaps the bride's bouquet, a gift certificate, or a small basket of treats.

Cultural traditions. Various cultures perform traditional activities during the reception, such as dancing the *hora* at a Jewish celebration, a Chinese bride changing outfits three times during the course of the party, the Greek *Kalamantiano* (or circle dance), the Polish "bridal capture," or the Italian "dollar dance."

Cutting the wedding cake. This traditional event may be scheduled at any time from the beginning of the reception to just before dessert is served. The bride and groom make the first, ceremonial cut of the cake, and feed each other. Let your master of ceremonies know how exactly you would like this handled—with an announcement and a special song played, or with little fanfare while the guests are being served their coffee.

Planning Your Reception

Worksheet 12: Outline for Master of Ceremonies & Musicians

Use this form as an outline for the emcee to follow. If you will not be including certain activities, simply cross them off with a large X. For those items you are including, fill out the pertinent information, and be sure to offer phonetic spellings for any names that might be difficult to pronounce. It is a good idea to give a copy of this outline not only to the bandleader but also to the maitre d', the photographer, and the videographer.

Cocktail hour

Time _____ to _____

Music _____

Introduction of bridal party

Give all names, in order, with relationship to bride and groom as needed.

Bride's parents _____

Groom's parents _____

Flower girl(s) _____

Ring bearer(s) _____

Bridal party (in order, you can have them come in individually or as couples)

_____

_____

_____

_____

_____

_____

_____

_____

Introduction of the bride and groom

This can be done as part of the bridal party introduction, or simply as a preface to the bride and groom's first dance. The emcee will typically preface the introduction with "For their first dance as husband and wife," but you should clarify any preferences you might have for the wording: Mr. and Mrs. John M. Smith, Mr. and Mrs. John and Mary Smith, John and Mary Smith, John Smith and Mary Jones.

Preferred introduction _____

First dance

Song _____ by _____

Ask other guests to join you on the dance floor? _____

Toasts

Give names of anyone you expect to give a toast. Indicate the person's relationship with you: sister, best man, old friend, etc.

_____

_____

_____

_____

Cutting of the cake

Announce it? _____

Music _____

Special music selections

Bride dances with father (or other)

_____

Groom dances with mother (or other)

_____

Ethnic music requests

_____

_____

_____

_____

Special dances

_____

_____

_____

_____

_____

Special songs

_____

_____

_____

_____

_____

Announcements

_____

_____

Other requests or restrictions

_____

_____

_____

_____

_____

Chapter Seven

Wedding Day Flowers

Whatever the style of your wedding, flowers play an integral part in setting the mood. You may have selected a site for your ceremony and reception that needs little adornment, or you may need to dress up the space to make it more festive. You will need flowers to adorn the members of the wedding party and centerpieces for the tables.

When interviewing floral designers, be prepared to tell them your wedding date and time, color scheme, budget, and flower preferences, if you have any. Convey the style of the wedding, and bring a picture of your gown and your bridesmaids' gowns. Ask if they are familiar with the location of your wedding, and if they have handled other affairs at that location. You will want to see photographs of the florists' work, and get references from other clients. Use **Worksheet 13** to help you plan all of the floral decorations you'll need for both ceremony and reception.

Cutting Flower Costs

Remember that flowers are expensive and will quickly add up. If you find yourself over budget, either cut back on the number of arrangements or see about handling some of the flowers yourself.

Shop around. Interview a few florists, and get estimates from each. Prices can vary a great deal, influenced by factors that have no bearing on your wedding, such as the neighborhood where the florist is located. Search out good, reputable florists, and don't be afraid to go to one a bit far from the wedding site; they may be willing to travel to get the extra business.

Seek alternatives. When you interview florists, show them what you like and ask if there are less costly alternatives that would look just as lovely. Try to stick to seasonal flowers—those that are in abundant supply around your wedding date. Not only will they be at their least expensive price of the year, but they'll also be the most seasonally appropriate decorations, and will be wonderfully fresh and fragrant.

Make your own decorations. Consider making your own decorations for the ceremony and reception sites. Pews and chairs can be decorated with bows of tulle or wide ribbon, which can be purchased in bulk and assembled long before the ceremony. For a few dollars per table, you can make lovely centerpieces for your reception with cut flowers or inexpensive potted plants.

Worksheet 13: Wedding Day Flowers

Decide what you want, and get estimates from more than one florist. You'll need to work with them to make some cuts or substitutions if you are still over budget. Some florists will agree to work out a package deal that includes all or most of your requirements at a set price.

Item	How many	Style	Estimated cost (1)	Estimated cost (2)
Personal flowers				
Bride's bouquet				
Toss-away bouquet				
Maid of honor's bouquet				
Bridesmaids' bouquets				
Flower girl's basket				
Mothers' and grandmothers' corsages				

Item	How many	Style	Estimated cost (1)	Estimated cost (2)
Groom's boutonnière				
Best man's and ushers' boutonnières				
Fathers' and grandfathers' boutonnières				
Floral hair wreaths or clips				
Ceremony site				
Floral arrangements				
Pews				
Altar				
Runner				

Item	How many	Style	Estimated cost (1)	Estimated cost (2)
Other				
Flower petals to be thrown				
Reception site				
Centerpieces for guest tables				
Arrangements for food and gift tables				
Flowers or plants for elsewhere at reception site				

Item	How many	Style	Estimated cost (1)	Estimated cost (2)
Flowers for cake and cake table				
Other decorations				
Rentals				

Chapter Eight

Capturing Your Memories

So many brides and grooms report that their wedding flew by and was over before they knew it. Seeing the photographs and videos from your wedding helps you to relive every wonderful moment, and both can become treasures that your children will some-day enjoy.

Photography

To ensure that you will be satisfied with the results, hire a professional photographer who specializes in weddings. Begin your search as early as possible—the best photographers can get booked up as much as a year in advance. As with your other wedding vendors, the best way to find a photographer is often by recommendation, but check the yellow pages and local bridal guides for advertisements. Telephone to check the photographer's availability and pricing, and if you feel you have a good lead, set up an appointment to review his or her portfolio.

There are many things that you should keep in mind when you meet with a potential photographer.

Style. Discuss the style of photographs that appeal to you. Do you want formal portraits, candids, or a combination of both? Do you like traditional wedding photos, or is a journalistic approach more to your liking? Will the photographer shoot in both color and black and white?

Consistency. When reviewing a portfolio, ask to see the pictures from an entire wedding, rather than a selection of the best shots from several weddings. Look for nice composition, coverage, and quality, as well as clearly focused and well-lit shots.

What's included. Find out exactly what you are contracting for. If contracting with a large studio, check that the photographer you interview is the one who will shoot your wedding. Understand how long he will be there—will he come early and stay late, or are you contracting for a set number of hours? Find out what's included in his standard package, and what the cost for extra prints is.

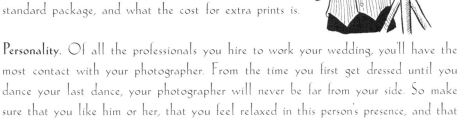

Personality. Of all the professionals you hire to work your wedding, you'll have the most contact with your photographer. From the time you first get dressed until you dance your last dance, your photographer will never be far from your side. So make sure that you like him or her, that you feel relaxed in this person's presence, and that you think you will enjoy spending the day in such close contact.

Videography

Many couples wish to have their wedding professionally captured on videotape as well as in still photographs. Some photography studios will also contract with you for the video, or you may have to find a separate videographer. When interviewing videographers, ask to see both edited and unedited versions of other wedding shoots. Observe the lighting, content, effects, and editing, and determine if the video is done in a style that you like.

Find out if there are any restrictions on photography or videography at your ceremony and reception sites, and pass the information along. Discuss the specifics of what you want covered, and prepare a list for each, using **Worksheet 15**. You may even want to discuss the photographer/videographer's attire on the day of your wedding. Include all details in your contract, including the names of the professionals who will do the work.

Worksheet 14: Finding a Photographer

Interview several photographers, and find out what they charge and what packages they offer. Some items, such as your album, may be included in the photographer's fee; note how many pages the album will have and how many shots per page.

Item	Photographer #1 _____ phone _____	Photographer #2 _____ phone _____
Color, black and white, or both?		
Photographer's fee		
Assistant's fee		
Shoot all day?		
Wedding album number of pages number of shots per page		
Estimated number of shots for day candids formals		

Capturing Your Memories

Item	Photographer #1 _____ phone _____	Photographer #2 _____ phone _____
Who keeps proofs?		
Parents' albums		

Prices for reprints
  wallet size
  4 x 6
  5 x 7
  8 x 10
  11 x 14
  other		

Other information		

Worksheet 15: Photography & Videography

Once you've made a decision on a photographer and videographer, keep track of pertinent information here. When hiring either a photographer or a videographer, be sure to check the contract to see if you can be refunded for work that is inacceptable or shots that are missed.

Photography

Name/studio _____

Address _____

_____

_____

Telephone _____

Number of assistants _____

Attire _____

Reserved date _____

Contract date _____

Time _____ to _____

Overtime fees _____

Deposit _____

Balance due _____

Additional fees _____

Time/location of arrival _____

Formal portraits to shoot _____

_____

_____

_____

_____

_____

Table shots _____

Events to shoot _____

_____

_____

_____

_____

_____

_____

Candid moments to shoot _____

_____

_____

Special family and friends _____

_____

_____

_____

_____

_____

Restrictions during ceremony _____

_____

_____

_____

_____

_____

Special effects _____

Proofs due/received _____

Selections made _____

Album ordered _____

Extra albums ordered _____

Extra proofs ordered _____

Disposable cameras for tables _____

Videography

Name/studio _____

Address _____

_____

Telephone _____

Number of assistants _____

Attire _____

Reserved date _____

Contract date _____

Time _____ to _____

Overtime fees _____

Deposit _____

Balance due _____

Additional fees _____

Time/location of arrival _____

Events to shoot _____

_____

_____

_____

_____

Candid moments to shoot _____

_____

_____

_____

_____

Special family and friends _____

_____

_____

_____

_____

_____

_____

Capturing Your Memories

Restrictions during ceremony _____

_____

_____

_____

_____

_____

_____

_____

Special effects _____

Primary viewing _____

Music selections for final edit _____

_____

_____

_____

Still photos for edit _____

_____

Final video due _____

Extra copies

_____

Additional fees _____

Chapter Nine

Getting Everyone There

From getting the groom to the church on time to finding a place to stay for out-of-town guests, transportation and travel plans are often a big part of a wedding. Planning ahead and shopping around are key to organizing the traffic on your wedding day.

Out-of-town Guests

Your guests will appreciate your help in locating accommodations. Many couples make arrangements with a local hotel to hold a block of rooms and may negotiate a group rate. Include a separate card with your invitation to alert guests to their options (see chapter three). Your guests will pay for their own lodging, even if you make the reservation for them.

If local friends and family offer to put up some out-of-town guests, accept the offer graciously and extend their invitation to guests who might have a hard time paying for both a hotel and airfare.

Plan to spend extra time with guests who have traveled to be with you—invite them to the rehearsal dinner, arrange activities to fill the unoccupied hours of the wedding day, host a brunch the following day to say good-bye to everyone. You might put together gift baskets—which could contain a map of the area, a schedule of events, bottled water, champagne, light snacks—and have them waiting in guests' rooms when they check in.

Getting Everyone There

Worksheet 16: Hotel Information

Note all the pertinent information on hotel accommodations for your guests here. Most hotels will have a specific date by which the hotel rooms need to be booked, be sure to remind your guests of it.

If your ceremony and reception sites are located far apart, or if you have many people staying at a hotel that is not near either, consider hiring a bus or van to pick up and drop off your guests. It will make things a lot easier for out-of-towners, will do away with the hassle of renting cars, and will eliminate the need for designated drivers.

Hotel _____

Phone _____

Concierge _____

Number of rooms reserved _____

Courtesy pickup from airport? _____

Dates reserved _____

Rate per room _____

Confirm by _____

It will make your life a lot easier if you create a map of your area that provides clear directions for anyone traveling to and from your wedding. Keep in mind that not only will guests need to find the ceremony and reception sites but your florist, photographer, caterer, band, and other professionals might need directions as well—and some of them will need directions to your home, and to and from the hotel, as well as to the wedding.

Arriving in Style

How you will get to your wedding is an important consideration if you're having it anywhere other than at home. There are as many ways to travel as there are ways to get married. Try to find the way that fits your style and your budget.

Driving yourself. Many people simply take their own cars to the wedding. This is certainly an option if you plan to change into your gown at the site, but could leave the bride and groom driving home separately after the celebration. Enlist a member of the bridal party to drive one of you or to bring one car home afterward. Remember that it is still customary in certain areas to "decorate" the bride and groom's car for their getaway after the reception. If you have any concerns, be sure to discuss them with your attendants.

Limousines. A limousine can be rented to take you to the ceremony, and from there to the reception. Many services charge by the hour, but it's possible to hire the car for the entire span of the reception as well. Find out if there is a minimum number of rental hours, what deposits are required as well as the form of payment, and if gratuities for the driver are included. If the balance of the fee is due on the wedding day, you might want to assign one of the attendants to take care of this for you.

Getting Everyone There

Check on insurance and licenses before hiring any company, discuss the driver's attire, and look at the cars themselves to confirm that they are in good condition. The contract should specify the car that you want. Use **Worksheet 17** to keep track of transportation specifics.

Other alternatives. Some brides and grooms choose to make a more splashy entrance and/or exit at their nuptial celebration. Consider vintage or classic cars, a horse-drawn carriage, even a hot-air balloon, sleigh, or boat. Whatever professional you choose to handle transportation, you should apply the same hiring criteria as with a limousine driver, noted above, when you interview them.

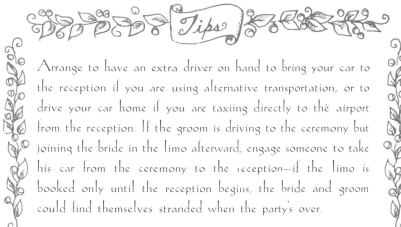

Tips

Arrange to have an extra driver on hand to bring your car to the reception if you are using alternative transportation, or to drive your car home if you are taxiing directly to the airport from the reception. If the groom is driving to the ceremony but joining the bride in the limo afterward, engage someone to take his car from the ceremony to the reception—if the limo is booked only until the reception begins, the bride and groom could find themselves stranded when the party's over.

 Worksheet 17: Transportation

Record all pertinent information regarding your transportation here.

Provider _____

Number of vehicles _____

Type(s) of vehicle(s) _____

Attire for driver _____

Reserved for _____ hours

Champagne? _____

Total cost _____

Deposit _____

Balance due _____ When? _____

Schedule

Pick up at (address) _____

_____

_____

_____

at _____ A.M./P.M.

Number of passengers _____

Arrive at ceremony (address) _____

_____

_____

_____

at _____ A.M./P.M.

Leave ceremony at approximately _____ A.M./P.M.

Getting Everyone There

Stops for photos _____

_____

_____

_____

Arrive at reception _____

_____

_____

_____

Leave reception _____

_____

_____

_____

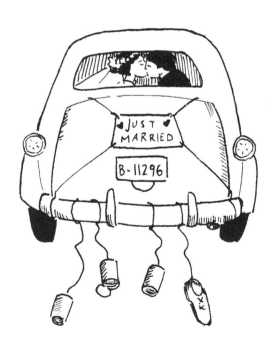

Chapter Ten

Gifts of Love

From the day you get engaged, you'll find yourselves the recipient of many gifts. Your friends and family, thrilled to see you embarking on this next phase of your life, will be thrilled to provide special tokens and useful items that will get you started on the right foot in your new married home.

Registering for Gifts

The bridal registry is a useful tool for engaged couples to indicate the items that they would enjoy receiving, making the gift-giving process much simpler for guests. Registering at department stores or specialty stores that have this kind of program is easy: go to the store, choose the items you would like to have, and the store keeps track of this list, usually under the bride's name, cross-referenced with the groom's.

When guests want to purchase gifts for you, they receive a copy of the list, including prices. Once an item is purchased, it is noted on the registry, thus avoiding duplication. The registry service is free to the couple and their guests, because the store earns its profit from the sale of the items. Most stores with bridal registries have the information computerized to keep better track of your list, especially for those stores that have more than one branch across the country. The bridal registry provides a win-win situation for the engaged couple and their guests. The couple can choose items that they need and want. The guests will be able to pick something in their price range that they know will be appreciated and not returned. Some stores will even wrap and ship the items to the bride and groom.

When to register. There are many schools of thought about when to register for gifts. The majority of couples register three to six months prior to the wedding, so that guests attending the bridal shower may select something from the registry if they choose. Other brides register shortly after their engagement. Typically, a bride and groom should not expect to receive engagement gifts, even if they have an engagement party. Nevertheless, there will be people close to you who want to buy a gift to celebrate your announcement, and if you are already registered, they can choose something that you have picked out.

Where to register. Look for stores that are convenient to all or most of your guests. If you have many guests coming from out of town, you might look for a store that has a mail-order catalog, a toll-free telephone number, or that will ship gifts free of charge. Check out their reputations for keeping registries up-to-date, and find out about their return policy.

You can register at more than one store, but don't register for the same items or you will end up with duplicates. Keep your registries to three or less, it may become too confusing after that. **Worksheet 18** will help keep you organized.

Tips

Make registry selections in various price ranges to give your guests a full range of options to fit their budgets. Some stores will allow you to register for generic gifts: you simply choose an item and give a little information about size and color preferences, and allow your guests to select something on their own. For example, you can register for sheets, queen size, pink or white, or register for a phone without stipulating what kind, and allow your guests to pick one they can afford.

The modern bride and groom are no longer bound by convention when it comes to registering—a couple who already have established households may not want the traditional items. Department stores supply a broad range of products for use throughout the home, from crystal and china to sheets and towels, while many catalog stores offer similar merchandise with convenient at-home shopping. Specialty stores are great for couples more interested in, for example, stocking a gourmet kitchen or creating a perfect garden, and independent local shops—including museum stores, art dealers, and antiques shops—also offer registries. Modern trends include registries at health spas, sporting goods stores, travel agents, even mortgage brokers.

Spreading the word. It is appropriate to include information about where you have registered on the invitation to your bridal shower, but not with your wedding invitation or announcements. In case they are asked by other guests, your closest family and friends should know where you are registered.

While many couples feel that they could make better use of a cash gift, traditional etiquette states that you should never tell your guests of this preference. On the other hand, passing this information to your parents or siblings and having them pass it on to inquiring guests is deemed appropriate. Nevertheless, no matter what your wishes, there will be some people who feel more comfortable giving a gift. And remember, your guests are not under any obligation to choose something from your registry—they may prefer to make their own selection.

Gifts of Love

Worksheet 18: Registering for Gifts

Shop around and decide on a store (or stores) that offers most of what you like and that is convenient to most of your guests. Use this chart to help you register for gifts and keep track of what you have received.

Most stores can provide you with a printout of your selections, and will update it for you as often as you like. Use this worksheet as a preliminary list to work out the colors for your rooms, or pattern preferences, and to remember everything when you go to register.

Dining Room

Formal china

Store _____

Pattern _____

Number of settings desired _____

Items to select:

    dinner plates _____

    salad plates _____

    soup bowls _____

    serving pieces _____

_____

_____

    other _____

_____

_____

Crystal

Store _____

Pattern _____

Number of settings desired _____

Items to select:

water goblets _____

white wine _____

red wine _____

brandy snifter _____

champagne flutes _____

other _____

_____

_____

Barware

Store _____

Pattern _____

Number of settings desired _____

Items to select:

highballs _____

rocks _____

cordials _____

other _____

_____

_____

Everyday china

Store _____

Pattern _____

Number of settings desired _____

Items to select:

dinner plates _____

salad plates _____

soup bowls _____

serving pieces _____

_____

_____

_____

other _____

_____

_____

Silverware

Formal pattern _____

number of settings _____

serving pieces _____

Everyday pattern _____

number of settings _____

serving pieces _____

Table linens

Store _____

Color preferences _____

_____

Style _____

Size of table _____

Items to select:

tablecloths _____

place mats _____

napkins _____

napkin rings _____

other _____

Kitchen

Cookware

Store _____

Manufacturer and brand _____

Items to select:

frying pans _____

stockpot _____

small saucepan _____

large saucepan _____

griddle _____

casserole _____

other _____

_____

_____

Appliances

Store _____

Items to select:

    microwave _____

    toaster _____

    blender _____

    food processor _____

    coffee maker _____

    phone _____

    other _____

_____

_____

Bedroom

Store _____

Bed size _____

Color and pattern _____

Items to select:

    comforter _____

    pillows _____

    dust ruffle _____

    pillow shams _____

    other _____

_____

_____

Bathroom

Store _____

Color preferences _____

Items to select:

shower curtain _____

hand towels _____

bath towels _____

bath sheets _____

bath mat _____

washcloths _____

accessories _____

_____

_____

_____

_____

Other Items

_____

_____

_____

_____

_____

_____

_____

_____

_____

_____

_____

_____

_____

_____

_____

_____

_____

_____

Chapter Eleven

Pre-Wedding Parties

As you are planning your wedding, you will find yourself being treated to many parties in your honor, and hosting many more to thank those who have supported you through the process.

Bridal Showers

According to traditional etiquette, the bridal shower should not be hosted by a member of your immediate family, as it may be seen as a plea for gifts. Of course, this is exactly what a shower is designed for, and why it developed in the first place. "Showering" the bride with gifts for her new home started as a means to expand the dowry of a bride-to-be from a family of modest means, thereby making her a more attractive "catch" to potential suitors. The parties were arranged and attended by the bride's friends to help her on her way, rather than cast any critical light on the family's assets.

The bride herself should have little if anything to do with the shower plans, although many wish to voice an opinion regarding the size or the style of the shower. You will have to supply your maid of honor with a guest list, and you should register well in advance so that guests are able to shop. The shower is centered around opening gifts, and you should send your thank-you notes promptly, as your schedule will get more and more hectic as the wedding approaches. To help you out with this, it's a good idea to have a bridesmaid or other friend make a list of each gift and who gave it to you as you open packages. You can use **Worksheet 19**, or your index-card file, to keep track.

Worksheet 19: Gift Log

Whenever you receive a gift, whether at your bridal shower or at home, promptly log it in, noting who it is from, what it is, and when it was received. (Alternatively, you can keep this information in your index-card file.) Send a thank-you note immediately, and log that in as well.

At your bridal shower, ask a friend to write down each gift along with the name(s) of its giver. This will make it much easier for you when you send your thank-you notes.

Name	Gift	Date received	Thank-you note sent

Name	Gift	Date received	Thank-you note sent

Name	Gift	Date received	Thank-you note sent

Name	Gift	Date received	Thank-you note sent

Pre-Wedding Parties

Name	Gift	Date received	Thank-you note sent

Name	Gift	Date received	Thank-you note sent

Pre-Wedding Parties

Bridesmaids' Party

As an expression of your appreciation for all their love and support, you may want to host a party for your attendants. Whether you take everyone out or invite them over is determined only by whatever idea appeals to you most. Have a tea, luncheon, brunch, or dinner, beer and pizza, coffee and cake, or truffles and champagne. Put together a gathering that reflects who you are and how you feel about the members of your wedding party, for this is your opportunity to thank them for their help and enjoy their company in a relaxed setting before the wedding.

The bridesmaids' party is usually held one or two weeks before the wedding. However, if you have out-of-town attendants, consider having a luncheon the day before to welcome them to town, or a breakfast or brunch the morning of the wedding.

In addition to the maid of honor and bridesmaids, invite your mother and future mother-in-law, your flower girl (and her mother), and other close female relatives, such as sisters and sisters-in-law. If your attitude is "the more, the merrier," you can even extend an invitation to any female guests who have come from out of town. Often, the bride will use this private moment to give her attendants their gifts. Of course, it's not required that this remain a "females only" event, if that doesn't suit your style.

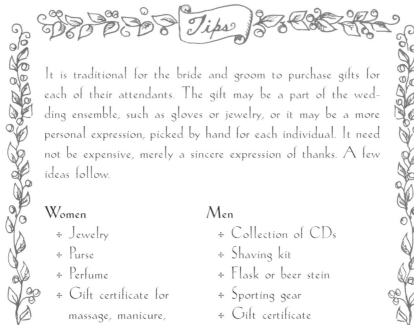

Tips

It is traditional for the bride and groom to purchase gifts for each of their attendants. The gift may be a part of the wedding ensemble, such as gloves or jewelry, or it may be a more personal expression, picked by hand for each individual. It need not be expensive, merely a sincere expression of thanks. A few ideas follow.

Women

+ Jewelry
+ Purse
+ Perfume
+ Gift certificate for massage, manicure, or facial

Men

+ Collection of CDs
+ Shaving kit
+ Flask or beer stein
+ Sporting gear
+ Gift certificate for massage

Worksheet 20: Bridesmaids' Party

Keep track of your plans and budget for your bridesmaids' party here.

Where
_____

Cost
_____

Contact
_____

Phone
_____

Date and time
_____
_____

Who attends
_____
_____
_____
_____
_____
_____
_____
_____
_____
_____
_____

Bachelor Party

The bachelor party is the traditional "final fling" for the groom—a night of revelry with his closest friends, which might be arranged by the best man, ushers, or close friends. It may be the only time during this entire process where the groom stands alone at the center of attention.

All male members of the bridal party are included, as well as other friends of the groom. The days of scantily clad women popping out of giant cakes are past, but many a modern stag party may still include some form of risqué entertainment. Yet

just as many may not—the groom who feels embarrassed or offended by such high jinks might prefer an evening of billiards, a day of golf, a late-night rock concert, or a simple dinner spent reminiscing with his friends and toasting his future bride.

If there will not be a rehearsal dinner, the groom may choose to give his attendants their gifts at the bachelor

party, and a quiet moment at the beginning of the evening may be the best opportunity. In the past this party was reserved for the night before the wedding, but now is usually held a week or two prior, avoiding the possibility of a hungover groom and groomsmen at the wedding itself.

Bachelorette Party

Not wanting to feel like she's missing out, many modern brides have bachelorette par-

ties these days that mirror the groom's big bash. Whether it's cocktails at the local jazz lounge, dancing at a singles' club, girls' night out at male strip shows, a grown-up slumber party, or a day of beauty at a salon or spa, the bride's bachelorette party should match her style rather than some cliché about stag parties.

Both the bride and groom should be careful to let their honor attendant know exactly how they feel about stag parties well in advance of the wedding.

Rehearsing for the Big Event

For anyone having a wedding with more than one attendant, a rehearsal can be a critical step in the ceremony running smoothly. Most rehearsals take place the night before or the morning of the wedding, because all the participants may not be able to gather before that time.

There are several people who may take charge at the wedding rehearsal: the officiant, the wedding coordinator, the banquet manager, even the bride. By this time you should already have discussed the critical details with everyone—your officiant knows what distinctive features you want to incorporate into the ceremony, the person or people escorting you down the aisle are aware of that role, etc. The rehearsal, therefore, is an actual walk-through of the ceremony, allowing everyone to practice what they will shortly be doing. For instance, ushers must know how to seat the guests, if there will be a bride's side and a groom's side, and if, how, and when they should release aisle runners and pew ribbons. Ushers must also be prepared to direct guests to the rest rooms, the coat rooms, and the reception. The bride should bring a practice bouquet—perhaps the bouquet made of ribbons from her shower—and a practice candle if there is to be a unity candle. This is the time to ensure that everyone understands his or her role, who follows whom in the processional and recessional, and most important, when all are supposed to arrive for the ceremony. Refer back to **Worksheet 10** for details.

Following a rehearsal the evening before the wedding, the participants (including clergy) may be invited to dinner. This party is customarily hosted by the groom's parents, but anyone may host it, including the bride and groom. Although some people enjoy having a formal rehearsal dinner, others prefer to have a very casual event in which they can relax before the activities of the wedding day. The spouses of attendants can also be included, as well as other close relatives or out-of-town guests.

Worksheet 21: Rehearsal Dinner

Keep track of the plans and budget for your rehearsal dinner here.

Where

_____

Cost

_____

Contact

_____

Phone

_____

Date and time

_____

Who attends

_____

_____

_____

_____

_____

_____

_____

_____

_____

_____

_____

_____

_____

Pre-Wedding Parties

Chapter Twelve

After the Wedding

When the hustle and bustle is over, the new husband and wife can kick off their shoes, relax, and enjoy some time alone together.

Take off for a honeymoon and enjoy it, because once you return it's back to work on the final important wedding details: sending thank-you notes, checking in with your photographer to view proofs, working with your videographer on editing, and setting up your new home.

The Honeymoon

As with every other issue surrounding weddings, there are different schools of thought about what to do on your honeymoon. For some, heading to a tropical island and being waited on hand and foot, with nothing more demanding than an afternoon of snorkeling, are just what is needed after the intense whirlwind surrounding the nuptials. Others take the opportunity to travel and sightsee. Couples who spend their vacations in active pursuit may feel that

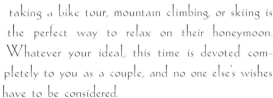

taking a bike tour, mountain climbing, or skiing is the perfect way to relax on their honeymoon. Whatever your ideal, this time is devoted completely to you as a couple, and no one else's wishes have to be considered.

If traveling to a foreign country, make sure your passport is valid, and check on special requirements such as visas or inoculations. If you are changing your name, be warned: don't make flight plans using your married name. This can cause serious problems, as your identification documents will show your maiden name, and these items can't be changed until after the wedding. If you don't have a passport, apply for one well in advance (it takes about a month or so to receive it once the application has been processed).

Worksheet 22: Honeymoon Details

After organizing the details of your trip, leave all the pertinent information with someone at home. Arrange for pickups and drop-offs at the airport, and if necessary, have someone drive your car home from the reception.

Accommodations for wedding night _____

Transportation for wedding night _____

Transportation to airport _____

Retrieve bride/groom's car _____

Travel itinerary

Leaving flight:

Leave _____ at _____

Arrive _____ at _____

Returning flight:

Leave _____ at _____

Arrive _____ at _____

Transportation from airport _____

Agenda while traveling

Make a list of locations where you'll be staying, and include phone numbers, for emergencies only. Leave the list with someone you trust who will respect your privacy.

Dates	Hotel	Emergency phone
_____	_____	_____
_____	_____	_____
_____	_____	_____

A Change in Status

When you return from your honeymoon, be prepared to make a few bureaucratic trips. If the bride plans on changing her name, see to it as soon as you return from your honeymoon. Even if you are keeping your maiden name, you'll still need to notify places like your payroll office, insurance carriers, and Social Security of your change in status regardless of whether or not you change your name.

Use the following checklist to make sure that the appropriate agencies and institutions are notified of your change in marital status and, if appropriate, your new name and your new address.

- [ ] Social Security
- [ ] Passport
- [ ] Driver's license
- [ ] Car registration(s)
- [ ] Auto insurance agent(s)
- [ ] Health insurance agent(s)
- [ ] Credit cards
- [ ] IRS
- [ ] Bank
- [ ] Payroll (bride and groom)

Newlywed Loose Ends

There are a number of post-wedding priorities that you'll need to follow up on as soon as you return from your honeymoon

Write your thank-you notes. It's best to thank people right away, not only as a matter of etiquette but because you'll still be filled with the excitement of the wedding and will simply write better and more heartfelt notes while the event—and the gift—is fresh in your mind.

Send wedding announcements. Many couples send out formal announcements to friends and family who were not invited to the wedding. You may also make announcements in your local newspapers and in your college or high school alumnae newsletters.

Check in with your photographer. Your proofs might be ready by the time you get back home. If you wish to enclose photographs with your thank-you notes, you'll need to pick them up in a timely fashion.

Follow up with the videographer. You'll need to review all edits and make certain they have all the extraneous materials—photographs, music, etc.—that they need.

Call the friends who couldn't make it. Get in touch with everyone who was unable to travel to your wedding, and share your thoughts on the day—and some photos, if possible—with them.

Make arrangements for your trousseau. You'll have tons of keepsakes, from your dried bouquet to your gown to the handkerchief you carried down the aisle. Have your wedding gown professionally cleaned and preserved, and put everything away in a special, secure place.

Hold on to your records. Invariably, other brides-to-be will call you asking for advice, contacts, and recommendations. Your wedding workbook will continue to be useful for years to come!

A Month-by-Month Planner

The many details that go into your wedding can be difficult to keep track of, and overwhelming to deal with all at once. This section of *The Wedding Workbook* breaks down all the details into a twelve-month calendar with simple to-do lists that will keep you in control and on top of everything. If you have less than a year to plan your wedding, just crunch the lists for the earlier months together, and by the time the wedding is just a few months away, you'll be right on schedule.

Twelve Months Before the Wedding

Month _____

Things to do:

+ Announce your engagement
+ Arrange for your families to meet
+ Discuss date, wedding style, and budget

CALENDAR

1. _____   17. _____
2. _____   18. _____
3. _____   19. _____
4. _____   20. _____
5. _____   21. _____
6. _____   22. _____
7. _____   23. _____
8. _____   24. _____
9. _____   25. _____
10. _____   26. _____
11. _____   27. _____
12. _____   28. _____
13. _____   29. _____
14. _____   30. _____
15. _____   31. _____
16. _____

Eleven Months Before the Wedding

Month _____

Things to do:
+ Estimate number of guests
+ Choose the members of your wedding party
+ Select and reserve ceremony and reception sites

CALENDAR

1. _____
2. _____
3. _____
4. _____
5. _____
6. _____
7. _____
8. _____
9. _____
10. _____
11. _____
12. _____
13. _____
14. _____
15. _____
16. _____

17. _____
18. _____
19. _____
20. _____
21. _____
22. _____
23. _____
24. _____
25. _____
26. _____
27. _____
28. _____
29. _____
30. _____
31. _____

Ten Months Before the Wedding

Month _____

Things to do:
+ Book consultant, caterer
+ Investigate and book officiant, photographer,
  videographer, and musicians for ceremony and reception

CALENDAR

1. _____
2. _____
3. _____
4. _____
5. _____
6. _____
7. _____
8. _____
9. _____
10. _____
11. _____
12. _____
13. _____
14. _____
15. _____
16. _____

17. _____
18. _____
19. _____
20. _____
21. _____
22. _____
23. _____
24. _____
25. _____
26. _____
27. _____
28. _____
29. _____
30. _____
31. _____

Nine Months Before the Wedding

Month _____

Things to do:
+ Shop for bridal gown
+ Register for gifts
+ Create guest list

CALENDAR

1. _____
2. _____
3. _____
4. _____
5. _____
6. _____
7. _____
8. _____
9. _____
10. _____
11. _____
12. _____
13. _____
14. _____
15. _____
16. _____

17. _____
18. _____
19. _____
20. _____
21. _____
22. _____
23. _____
24. _____
25. _____
26. _____
27. _____
28. _____
29. _____
30. _____
31. _____

Eight Months Before the Wedding

Month _____

Things to do:
+ Discuss honeymoon plans
+ Book florist
+ Shop for bridal accessories: shoes, veil, underpinnings
+ Shop for bridesmaids' dresses

CALENDAR

1. _____
2. _____
3. _____
4. _____
5. _____
6. _____
7. _____
8. _____
9. _____
10. _____
11. _____
12. _____
13. _____
14. _____
15. _____
16. _____

17. _____
18. _____
19. _____
20. _____
21. _____
22. _____
23. _____
24. _____
25. _____
26. _____
27. _____
28. _____
29. _____
30. _____
31. _____

Seven Months Before the Wedding

Month _____

Things to do:

+ Shop for attire for groom and groomsmen
+ Discuss details with caterer and reception manager
+ Order invitations and other stationery
+ Reserve rooms at hotel for out-of-town guests

CALENDAR

1. _____   17. _____
2. _____   18. _____
3. _____   19. _____
4. _____   20. _____
5. _____   21. _____
6. _____   22. _____
7. _____   23. _____
8. _____   24. _____
9. _____   25. _____
10. _____   26. _____
11. _____   27. _____
12. _____   28. _____
13. _____   29. _____
14. _____   30. _____
15. _____   31. _____
16. _____

Six Months Before the Wedding

Month _____

Things to do:
+ Meet with officiant to discuss the ceremony
+ Discuss details with florist
+ Finalize honeymoon plans
+ Make arrangements for time off from work

CALENDAR

1. _____
2. _____
3. _____
4. _____
5. _____
6. _____
7. _____
8. _____
9. _____
10. _____
11. _____
12. _____
13. _____
14. _____
15. _____
16. _____

17. _____
18. _____
19. _____
20. _____
21. _____
22. _____
23. _____
24. _____
25. _____
26. _____
27. _____
28. _____
29. _____
30. _____
31. _____

Five Months Before the Wedding

Month _____

Things to do:
+ Discuss details with musicians,
  photographer, videographer
+ Shop for wedding favors
+ Reserve rental equipment

CALENDAR

1. _____
2. _____
3. _____
4. _____
5. _____
6. _____
7. _____
8. _____
9. _____
10. _____
11. _____
12. _____
13. _____
14. _____
15. _____
16. _____

17. _____
18. _____
19. _____
20. _____
21. _____
22. _____
23. _____
24. _____
25. _____
26. _____
27. _____
28. _____
29. _____
30. _____
31. _____

Four Months Before the Wedding

Month _____

Things to do:
+ Finalize the guest list, and confirm addresses as needed
+ Check local requirements for marriage license and blood tests
+ Arrange transportation for wedding day

CALENDAR

1. _____
2. _____
3. _____
4. _____
5. _____
6. _____
7. _____
8. _____
9. _____
10. _____
11. _____
12. _____
13. _____
14. _____
15. _____
16. _____

17. _____
18. _____
19. _____
20. _____
21. _____
22. _____
23. _____
24. _____
25. _____
26. _____
27. _____
28. _____
29. _____
30. _____
31. _____

Three Months Before the Wedding

Month _____

Things to do:

- Arrange rehearsal and rehearsal dinner
- Order wedding rings
- Finalize floral arrangements
- Write out and stuff invitations
- Make arrangements with a moving company, if necessary
- Go for wedding gown fitting

CALENDAR

1. _____
2. _____
3. _____
4. _____
5. _____
6. _____
7. _____
8. _____
9. _____
10. _____
11. _____
12. _____
13. _____
14. _____
15. _____
16. _____

17. _____
18. _____
19. _____
20. _____
21. _____
22. _____
23. _____
24. _____
25. _____
26. _____
27. _____
28. _____
29. _____
30. _____
31. _____

Two Months Before the Wedding

Month _____

Things to do:

+ Mail your invitations and begin tracking responses
+ Finalize reception menu
+ Order wedding cake
+ Arrange attendants' luncheon
+ Write or choose your vows
+ Create a "play" list for musicians, photo list for photographer
+ Purchase gifts for attendants
+ Begin packing to move, if necessary
+ Pick up your wedding gown

CALENDAR

1. _____
2. _____
3. _____
4. _____
5. _____
6. _____
7. _____
8. _____
9. _____
10. _____
11. _____
12. _____
13. _____
14. _____
15. _____
16. _____

17. _____
18. _____
19. _____
20. _____
21. _____
22. _____
23. _____
24. _____
25. _____
26. _____
27. _____
28. _____
29. _____
30. _____
31. _____

One Month Before the Wedding

Month _____

Things to do:

+ Send announcements to newspapers
+ Call all vendors to confirm arrangements
+ Confirm honeymoon arrangements
+ Get a haircut and facial, test hairdos
  with your veil
+ Break in your wedding shoes
+ Create ceremony program
+ Check on name/status change requirements
+ Obtain marriage license
+ Send out change of address forms,
  if necessary

CALENDAR

1. _____
2. _____
3. _____
4. _____
5. _____
6. _____
7. _____
8. _____
9. _____
10. _____
11. _____
12. _____
13. _____
14. _____
15. _____
16. _____

17. _____
18. _____
19. _____
20. _____
21. _____
22. _____
23. _____
24. _____
25. _____
26. _____
27. _____
28. _____
29. _____
30. _____
31. _____

One Week Before the Wedding

Dates _____

Things to do:

+ Create the seating plan and write out place cards
+ Pack your honeymoon bag
+ Confirm the final number of guests with the caterer
+ Host your attendants' luncheon
+ Make a list of items that must be brought home from the reception

+ Create schedule of events for the wedding day
+ Review with everyone what their jobs are
+ Make gift baskets to leave in hotel rooms for out-of-town guests
+ Write toasts
+ Address wedding announcements
+ Confirm details with vendors

SCHEDULE

Saturday _____
_____

Sunday _____
_____

Monday _____
_____

Tuesday _____
_____

Wednesday _____
_____

Thursday _____
_____

Friday _____
_____

The Day Before Your Wedding

Date _____

Things to do:

+ Get a manicure and pedicure
+ Pack emergency kit and other items, such as guest book and pen
+ Confirm travel arrangements for honeymoon
+ Confirm wedding-day transportation

+ Finalize seating plan
+ Attend the rehearsal and rehearsal dinner
+ Give gifts to the wedding party, if not already done
+ Get a good night's rest

SCHEDULE

8:00 A.M. _____

_____

9:00 A.M. _____

_____

10:00 A.M. _____

_____

11:00 A.M. _____

_____

12:00 P.M. _____

_____

1:00 P.M. _____

_____

2:00 P.M. _____

_____

3:00 P.M. _____

_____

4:00 P.M. _____

_____

5:00 P.M. _____

_____

6:00 P.M. _____

_____

7:00 P.M. _____

_____

8:00 P.M. _____

_____

9:00 P.M. _____

_____

10:00 P.M. _____

_____

11:00 P.M. _____

_____

Additional Resources

Bride's magazine offers information on every aspect of wedding planning, from style to etiquette to honeymoon ideas. Published bimonthly, it is available at newsstands and through subscription (call 800-456-6162 for information).

Elegant Bride magazine is dedicated to helping brides-to-be plan elegant, timeless weddings. Published four times per year, it is available through newsstands and subscriptions (call 336-378-6065 for information). The magazine is also available on the internet (www.elegantbride.com).

Modern Bride magazine offers everything for today's bride, from wedding fashions to home fashions. The magazine is published bimonthly, and is available through subscription (call 800-777-5786 for information) and at newsstands. The magazine also maintains a useful website (www.modernbride.com).

The Knot (www.theknot.com) is a popular wedding planning website that offers fashion tips, etiquette rules, and ideas in an easily searchable format. Chat rooms and mailing lists put you in touch with other brides.

The Wedding Channel (www.weddingchannel.com) offers tons of wedding planning information in an easily searchable format.

Town & Country magazine offers a great wedding issue, and the magazine maintains a terrific wedding-only website (www.tncweddings.com).

Wedding Bells (www.weddingbells.com) is a unique website that focuses on wedding planning for both American and Canadian brides.

Index